Marijuana:

It's an Herb with an Asterisk

By

Jack Isler MD

DORRANCE
PUBLISHING CO
EST. 1920
PITTSBURGH, PENNSYLVANIA 15238

Dorrance Publishing Co
585 Alpha Drive
Pittsburgh, PA 15238
Visit our website at *www.dorrancebookstore.com*

ISBN: 978-1-4809-3269-2
eISBN: 978-1-4809-3292-0

Contents

Illustrations

Figures

Tables

Introduction

Marijuana can be referred to as cannabis, pot, reefer, buds, grass, weed, dope, ganja, the herb, boom, gangster, Mary Jane, sinsemilla, shit, joint, hash, hash oil, blow, blunt, green, kilobricks, Thai sticks, etc. Specifically, marijuana refers to the leaves and the flowering tops of the cannabis plant. Marijuana has a broad spectrum of effects, including stimulation, sedation, hallucination, tranquilization, and anti-inflammation. Some say it is the most commonly used illicit drug in the world. Twenty-three states have medical marijuana programs, and four states passed legislation to permit recreational and medical use as of 2015. Is it illicit, or not? Reportedly, 40% of Canadians have used marijuana at some point in their life, while about 25 million people use it at least once a year in the U.S. More education about marijuana will return it to its herbal status. Marijuana's status changed when the FDA classified is as a Schedule I drug in 1970.

I have been using cannabis products for over forty years. Initially, I had used it recreationally before I used marijuana and its products for chronic pain relief. Until the last few years,

I had kept my use of these products very private because I wanted to avoid legal ramifications as a result of having been a professional physician. As an ICU physician, I used synthetic forms of THC for patient care as needed. As I neared retirement, having finished a book on chronic pain, it seemed a good time to defend cannabis for what it is: an herb of amazing potential. It is an herb that needs an asterisk, not a Schedule I drug classification.

I intentionally kept this book to a length that can be read in several short sittings. It is a handbook for the masses. To get the FDA to change the status of marijuana, millions of knowledgeable people will need to inundate them with messages of change. After you read this book, you should be able to make an intelligent decision about using marijuana for medical or recreation purposes. From the basic chemical presentation, to an in-depth typing of the marijuana plant—you will understand what marijuana actually is, instead of what it may represent to some. The discussion points are followed by scientific evidence; if there is no real evidence, then this will also be clear. The most common medical uses of marijuana are discussed at length, some of which are not simple to discuss because they are not simple topics. You do not need to understand all of the science to understand marijuana. The legal and professional ramifications of the use of marijuana are always a misunderstood concern. The federal government should step out of the way and let the states handle cannabis. The FDA has not handled marijuana as it should, and it might be too late to change the consequences. If marijuana were to regain its herbal status, it would not be under the FDA. Several chapters are devoted to answering legal types of questions, such as, which lab tests are accurate and how long does the effect of marijuana last?

Secondary effects of marijuana on fetuses and adolescents have some clear answers. The separation between the medical and the political arguments about marijuana lead to discussions about its being a gateway drug—or not—for more harmful drugs. One goal is to separate fact from fiction.

Marijuana's future is not only up to our physicians and suppliers, but also its users. Education and knowledge will give us the answers and the power we need for change. Being negative just to be negative will not cut it anymore. The theme of marijuana's helpful and enjoyable nature continues throughout the book.

.

Chapter One
The Cannabis Plant: History, Different Species, Hybrids, and Chemical Composition

All of your preconceived notions about marijuana (from the cannabis plant) need to be placed on hold. The following chapters will clarify that marijuana is not "the unknown" despite the way many like to present it. Thousands of articles and research papers have been written about marijuana. It was first thought to be grown over 4,500 years ago. Archeologists found it in the grave of a Chinese shaman that is 2,700 years old; it was used for medicinal and psychoactive purposes. In 400 CE, cannabis was cultivated in England. The British started cultivating cannabis in Virginia in 1611 CE, which was used for bartering. The Declaration of Independence was drafted on cannabis paper. In 1938, research was done to clarify the active principles of cannabis resin. In 1939, the Annals of Internal Medicine stated, "There is a wave of addiction to smoking of marijuana cigarettes in various parts of the United States." A symposium in 1971 at Stockholm, Sweden, was headed by US VA physician Dr. Leo Hollister. The discussion centered on the chemistry, biologic activity, and pharmacokinetics of cannabinoids—active chemicals in cannabis, such as THC and CBD. Forty papers were presented at this symposium alone. There were over one hundred new research papers in 2014-2015. Several publications devoted their entire monthly issues, which consisted of over a dozen new research articles, to the topic of marijuana. Let's discover what we know about cannabis and marijuana.

The terminology of some aspects of cannabis needs to be clarified first. Cannabis is a plant and an herb. Its leaves and flowers are where marijuana comes from. Cannabis has a high-growing version that is most commonly referred to as hemp. Hemp has a low THC (tetrahydrocannabinol) content, the chemical which affects the mind. It is used for hemp seed oil, wax, resin, rope, cloth, pulp, paper, and fuel. Cannabis also has a low-growing version with high levels of THC content. There are three basic sub species of this low growing version of cannabis. These three species are *Cannabis indica, Cannabis sativa*, and *Cannabis ruderalis.* The crossbreeding of these three sub-species yields a wide variety of hybrid strains, which all have unique characteristics. Until recently, it was thought there were three species of cannabis, which was concluded using genomes in a complete DNA study that were all actually from the same species. *C. sativa* was actually *C. indica*, which originated in India; *C. indica* was actually *C. afghanica*, which originated in Afghanistan; and *C. ruderalis* was mistaken for *C. sativa*. Using these new names to correct erroneous taxonomy might take some time. I will use the correct taxonomy here as much as possible. The principal does not change.

Indica (formerly sativa) plants are tall and loosely-branched and have long, narrow leaves. They are easily grown outdoors, and they can grow to twenty feet. *C. afghanica* (formerly indica) plants are short and have dense branches and wide leaves. They are more of an indoor plant. Appearances aside, the effect of these plants is what intrigues us. *Cannabis indica* has an uplifting, energetic purpose and a "cerebral, hallucinogenic" center. It is thought to be better suited for the daytime. *C. afghanica* is more relaxing and calming. It is best suited for nighttime use. The original classification of *Cannabis indica* (now *afghanica*) in 1785 distinguished Indian cannabis from European cannabis, which was *C. sativa* at the time.

The difference between *C. indica* and *C. afghanica* has a genetic origin. Due to different enzyme-proliferation, plants end up with high THC: CBD ratios, such as *C. indica*, or high CBD: THC ratios, such as *C. afghanica*; CBD is cannabidiol and THC is tetrahydrocannabinol. This is all strictly from a pure point of view. There are so many strains today that the genetic expression of the original plants is diluted and not as species-specific as before. Geographical origins and the plant's genome show there was just one cannabis species originally.

Indica leaf   Sativa leaf

Figure 1 Sativa (Indica) and Indica (Afghanica)

Afghanica strains grow and mature faster than indica strains because they have more chlorophyll. Pure strains of indica and afghanica can be combined with numerous hybrid stains, which should yield an infinite number of different hybrids. These hybrids could grow, mature, and be smoked at a rate commiserate with the percentage of indica and afghanica. These new hybrids could match the demand of consumers. In the future, we might be able to better match a patient's medical needs to a specific hybrid.

Pure indica is a rarity, especially in medical marijuana. It is hard to cultivate, and it does not fit an indoor venue because it can grow to be twenty-feet. After it begins to flower, it can take up to sixteen weeks until it reaches full maturity. Pure indica is rarely used for medical purposes because it can cause paranoid reactions and irregular heartbeats. In spite of this, pure indica has been used for severe depression and chronic fatigue. The seeds of this plant are valued highly by growers for their genetic stability. This plant is more likely to come from Columbia, Mexico, or Southeast Asia.

Pure afghanica comes from countries that produce large amounts of hash: Pakistan, Afghanistan, Tibet, and Morocco. After flowering starts, these plants mature in six-to-eight weeks. They are ideal for growing indoors because of their shorter stature. Cannabis afghanica was recognized as medicinal by the West in the early 1800's.

Cannabis sativa is a wilder version of cannabis. Its flowering time is short but variable. Flowering may be independent of the sun's cycles. Its wild nature makes it more resistant to frost. CBD is more prominent than THC. THCa (tetrahydrocannabinolic acid) is part of the plant, but it changes to THC. We will just refer to it as THC for clarity.

What is marijuana? Speaking from a scientific point of view, marijuana constitutes the dried flowers, leaves, stems, and seeds of the cannabis plant, which contain the chemicals and compounds that produce a recreational high or pain relief. The DEA stated in 2006 that marijuana is the most commonly-used illicit drug in the United States. Marijuana is a Schedule I substance under the Controlled Substances Act (initiated in 1970). Schedule I drugs are classified as having a high potential for abuse. They aren't currently acceptable for medical treatment or considered safe for use in the United States. The DEA definition contrasts with the twenty-three states that currently recognize medical marijuana as a necessity (the first of which was California in 1995) and the four states that have legalized recreational and medical marijuana. In 1988, a federal judge thought that marijuana should be reclassified as a Schedule II drug. The FDA said no in 1988, 2001, and 2006. It remains to be sorted out as to who will control the legal use of marijuana. A full discussion of this will take place in Chapter 11: The Law and Marijuana.

The chemical composition of cannabis starts with the seed. 100 grams of seed is approximately 13% water, 27% protein, 26% carbohydrate, 25% fat, and 20% fiber. There is also calcium, phosphorus, iron, beta-carotene, thiamine, riboflavin, niacin, cannabinoids, steroids, hydrocarbons, terpenes (which is responsible for the smell), flavonoids, and simple alcohols, which adds up to 400Kcals. Seed oil is 25-35% oil, and it is low in saturated fats, which make up only 10%. This oil contains saturated and unsaturated fats. These numbers are an average representation of a cannabis seed.

The chemicals in cannabis are clearly our focus when we speak of marijuana. There are over 400 chemicals in the cannabis plant. At this time, about eighty of these chemicals are unique to the cannabis plant. These are called cannabinoids. The cannabinoids have been divided into ten subclasses. Several of these are pharmacologically active. The exact number of relevant chemicals is unknown. This lack of understanding may explain why isolated chemicals thought to produce a certain level of action are not as strong or consistent as if they were part of a group of chemicals. There may a synergistic action between the chemicals. THC is the lead chemical.

Classes of Cannabinoids

1. Cannabigerol (first cannabinoids identified)—had some antibiotic properties
2. Cannabichromene (CBC)—antibiotic, antifungal, analgesic
3. Cannabidiol—CBD—anti-inflammatory, anti-spasmodic
4. Delta 9 tetrahydrocannabinol—euphoriant, anti-oxidant, anti-emetic
5. Delta 8 tetrahydrocannabinol—similar to delta 9 THC but less potent
6. Cannabicyclol—heat derived from CBC
7. Cannabielsoin—formed from CBD
8. Cannabinol—oxidation of THC and CBD—concentration depends on age and storage of the plant
9. Cannabitriol—only reported ester compound of the cannabinoids
10. Misc. cannabinoids—there are eleven of these currently identified

Talking about the major cannabinoids and separating them from the minor cannabinoids will simply things. There are two basic THCs, delta 9 and delta, of which there are almost a dozen variants. Delta 9 THC is much more abundant than delta 8 THC. There are five other non-minor chemicals, which include tetrahydrocannabitriol, cannabichromene (CBC), cannabidiol (CBD), cannabinol that forms after the plant dies (CBN), and THC acids A and B, which are inactive unless smoked; all of these have multiple variants. This gives us another look at why separate chemicals may not be as strong or powerful as ones in an intact plant system. Most of the research and focus for medical or recreational effects pertain to THC and CBD.

THC has a tricyclic 21 carbon structure. It is a volatile, viscous oil, which is very lipid-soluble with little water solubility. CBD is also a 21 carbon structure and a viscous oil with low water-solubility. THC is very light-sensitive and can decompose. Under acid conditions (not found in the human body), CBD can cyclize (undergo a reaction) to THC.

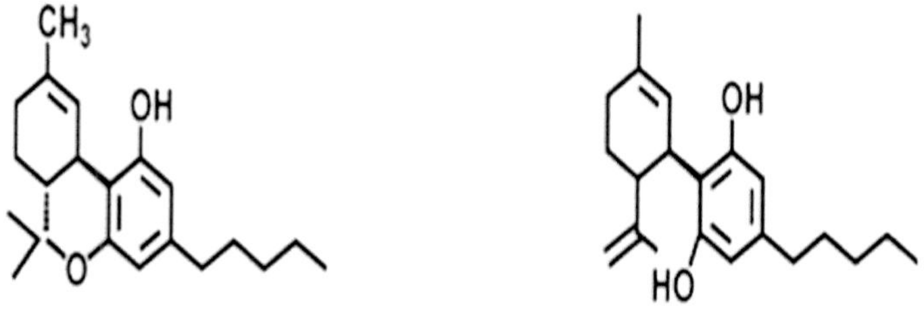

Δ^9-tetrahydrocannabinol (THC)

Cannabidiol (CBD)

Figure 2 Chemical Structure of THC and CBD

Cannabinoids are produced in the epidermal glands on the leaves, stems, and bracts, all of which support the flowers of the cannabis plant. The flowers themselves have no epidermal glands, but they have the highest cannabinoid content of the plant. This is due to the concentrated resin at the base of the flower. Basically, THC is created when a plant-precursor chemical—a cannabolic acid—loses a carboxyl group (COOH) as a result of sunlight, cooking, or smoking. THC was first artificially synthesized in 1964, and a synthetic version called marinol was approved by the FDA in 1985.

There are many metabolites of the cannabinoids, particularly THC; it seems as if the total effect of THC is related to itself and all these breakdown products. The effects of THC might be more complete if it were evaluated in the context of all the cannabinoids instead of a pure form. The anti-nausea effects of THC on nausea caused by chemotherapy are more effective when the patient intakes THC via a marijuana cigarette as compared to marinol (synthetic THC).

The levels of THC in marijuana ranges from 1.4% (a minor amount) to 33% (a high amount). On average, hashish and hash oil are 52% and 47% THC respectively. The increase in the percentage of THC in marijuana over the last decade is remarkable and scary. It appears to be consumer-driven, and it has a much higher risk-ratio. Commercially, several factors are responsible: progress in breeding techniques, cultivation in indoors, and access to a worldwide network of seeds and plants. Most of the THC in commercial hemp comes from contamination by seeds. There should be little to no THC in hemp if seeds are clean and quality-control is adequate.

The non-cannabinoid chemicals also merit discussion. The scent associated with cannabis comes from 140 different terpenes/terpenoids. Terpenoids are acyclic, monocyclic, and polycyclic hydrocarbons; all are part of the essential oils of most plants. Cannabinoids originate from a terpenoids structure. Terpenoids can be extracted in an oil format, and they are used in candles and other fragrance modalities. Cannabis terpenoids have antibiotic, anti-inflammatory properties, and they are sometimes used in herbal remedies. They can also make a plant more aromatic or taste when they are manipulated to increase their terpene content. In THC extractions, most of the terpenes have already been burnt off. Some evidence indicates terpenes increase the high resulting from THC, allowing lower THC percentages.

There are twenty-three commonly-occurring flavonoids in cannabis; two of these, cannflavins A and B, are unique to cannabis. Flavonoids have strong antioxidant properties, and they can be used to defend the human body against multiple ailments, including some cancers. Studies that use marijuana to assist against some forms of cancer are ongoing.

Chapter One Summary

- When using correct taxonomy, *Cannabis sativa* is actually *Cannabis indica*, *Cannabis indica* is actually *Cannabis afghanica*, and *Cannabis ruderalis* is actually *Cannabis sativa*; it makes little difference because of massive amounts of cross-breeding.
- Hemp also comes from a cannabis plant, but it has little to no THC content; it can be used for clothing, ropes, paper, and many other things.
- There are many cannabinoids (around eighty), but the two that intrigue us the most are THC (tetrahydrocannabinol) and CBD (cannabidiol).
- There are many other oils that are part of the cannabis plant; many of these are also used in medicine and, cooking, such as the terpenes/terpenoids and flavonoids.
- Marijuana was made a Schedule I drug in 1970; several times, in 1988, 2001, and 2006, the FDA refused to change the status of marijuana.

Chapter Two
Cannabinoid System and Receptors

This chapter is significantly more complex. It is important to read—if not more than once—to get a feel for how complicated marijuana's interaction with our body is. This is an evolving science because of this complexity. The cannabinoids and their subsequent receptors control so many aspects of our physiology that a rudimentary knowledge of them is necessary.

In 1990, Herkenham mapped out the locations of a cannabinoid (endocannabinoid) system in man; these would be the receivers (or receptors) for the cannabinoids from the marijuana and the body's own cannabinoids. Interestingly, the human body has receptors for specific plant chemicals, which are cannabinoids in this case. They target key protein receptors and interact with key physiological systems. Some say that the endocannabinoid system (ECS) is the most important system for maintaining health. It definitely is involved in dozens of bodily functions.

These cannabinoid receptors reach maximum density in the basal ganglia, hippocampus, and the cerebellum, which are parts of the brain. There are none of these cannabinoid receptors in the medulla, which is the cardio-respiratory center of the brain. This might explain why there are very few fatal overdoses from marijuana. The location and density of these receptors suggests they are involved with cognition and movement. The basal ganglia and the cerebellum modulate motor control, somewhat assuring that correct motor commands are sent to lower levels of the brain and spinal cord.

In Figure 4, we see that presynaptic stimulation from THC can lead to postsynaptic formation of cannabinoids. This is one of the ways intrinsic or extrinsic cannabinoids can lead to formation of more cannabinoids. This can then lead to modulation (or regulation) of many systems.

The effect of cannabis is extensive in the human body because of its cannabinoid content. This relates to the human endocannabinoid system. Although the endogenous cannabinoid system reaches maximum density in the brain, it is also found in organs, connective tissue, glands, and immune cells. From a holistic point of view, it seems as if the goal of the endocannabinoid system (ECS) is homeostasis. Homeostasis is essentially the goal of a system—in this case the body—of regulating variables, or to assure internal conditions remain constant while external conditions change. This endocannabinoid system is involved with appetite, pain, mood, memory, movement, and possibly the oversight of cell death and disposal. Perhaps, in a context of homeostasis, the cannabinoids attack tumor cells and thereby promote a patient's survival.

Cannabinoid receptors are a class of cell membrane receptors. These receptors are of the G protein-coupled receptor superfamily. A signal is sensed outside the cell and then an internal reaction takes place. There are many different transmitters for this system, and in this case, the transmitter is a cannabinoid, either one produced by the body or an external source.

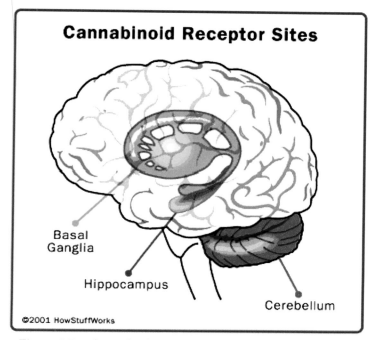

Figure 3 Basal ganglia, hippocampus, cerebellum of the brain

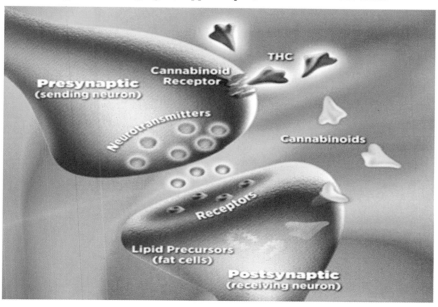

Figure 4 Post synaptic effects of cannabinoids

There are two known subtypes of the cannabinoid receptors: CB 1 and CB 2. CB 1 is mostly found in the brain/central nervous system and CB 2 is mostly found in the immune/blood systems. CB 1 and CB 2 have a significant amount of structural similarities. Depending on the part of the structure that is being examined, 40-60% of these receptors are identical. There are other novel cannabinoid receptors: GPR55, GPR 18, GPR 119, and VR 1 (also known as the capsaicin receptor). The GPR55, GPR18, and GPR 119, are G protein-coupled receptors, as are the CB receptors; but they are not as densely expressed or diverse in its effects as the CB 1 and CB 2 receptors. The VR1 (or TRPV1) is a transient receptor cation channel member that stops giving out pain signals when blocked. This antagonism can be the result of cannabinoids or capsaicin. We will mostly focus on CB1 and CB 2 receptors.

Capsaicin is a natural component found in spicy peppers. It is used as a topical ointment to relieve pain. There is an initial burning sensation, and then the pain will disappear. Capsaicin works on the VR1 receptors exactly as a cannabinoid does.

The cannabinoid receptor 1, or the CB 1, is one of the most common G protein-coupled receptors in the brain. This goes along with effects noted from marijuana. The body's endocannabinoids are very actively modulating neurotransmissions in the brain. In the liver, the endocannabinoids work on a CB 1 receptor and increase lipogenesis (putting fat in storage); these chemical sequences are beyond the scope of this book. CB 2 receptors are located in the T-cells, B-cells, and macrophages of the blood/immune system. They are also located on peripheral nerves. Some CB 2 receptors are present in the brain, but they do not have a known function at this time. Based on their location, the CB 2 receptors appear to have a large role in pain relief; this might result from downregulation of cytokine production and upregulation of regulatory T-cells, which decrease inflammation.

THC (tetrahydrocannabinol) and CBD (cannabidiol) are two of the main cannabinoids in cannabis. THC interacts with both main cannabinoid receptors, but CBD does not as long it isn't in extreme physiologic doses. CBD probably interacts with the novel cannabinoid receptors described above.

The many effects of all the cannabinoids seemingly extend past the CB 1 and CB 2 receptors. Several effects accomplished by cannabinoids do not have CB 1 or CB 2 receptors in the area. These other receptors have yet to be clearly identified, but they clearly are physiologically present.

The body's own cannabinoids merit a brief inclusion. The two main ones are anandamide and 2-arachidonylglycerol (2-AG). They have the ability to be synthesized on demand, a local impact, and a very short half-life. Our understanding of this system allows us to see the possible link between our mind and our body. This link can promote our health. External cannabinoids can aid in social interactions by potentially promoting learning, sharing, and creativity. Is it possible that the cannabinoids of marijuana can be a preventative medicine?

There are some non-cannabinoid plant chemicals that interact with the cannabinoid receptors. These are defined as phytocannabinoids; for example, terpenes have an affinity for CB 2 receptors. In most cases, they are currently used as food additives, but they have the potential for pain relief and a strong anti-inflammatory effect upon interaction with the CB 2 receptor.

The interaction between the central and peripheral endocannabinoid systems and their effects on body weight and composition are being studied. Some evidence suggests that over-activation of the CB 1 receptors leads to increased abdominal-obesity (fat deposition) and reduced insulin-responsiveness in skeletal muscles. There is also an increase in appetite that promotes food-seeking behavior. The opposite occurs when the partial CB 2 receptor or novel receptor-activator CBD is given. There are many situations where a CB 2 activation might block a CB 1 activation. Usually, CBD has few CB1/CB 2 activation properties. The point is if we optimize the tone of the endocannabinoid system, then we also optimize our body's ability to function.

Chapter Two Summary

- In 1990, the body's own cannabinoid system was mapped out; the cannabinoids of marijuana fit on our cannabinoid receptors and our body produces its own cannabinoids.
- The cannabinoid receptors reach maximum density in the brain.
- The endocannabinoid system (our body's own system) is involved in homeostasis.
- There are two main cannabinoid receptors: CB 1 and CB 2; there are also several other novel cannabinoid receptors throughout the body.
- The two main cannabinoids of marijuana are THC and CBD. The two main cannabinoids that our body produces are anandamide and 2-arachidonylglycerol.
- The endocannabinoid system gives us a direct link between our mind and our body. Optimization of the tone of the cannabinoid system will optimize our body's ability to function.

Chapter Three
Pharmacokinetics of Cannabinoids

As with all drugs/medications, we must understand their pharmacokinetics; this is their unique characteristics associated with deposition, breakdown, and excretion. Pharmacokinetics provides knowledge about the time a drug takes to reach the onset of its effect and the duration and magnitude of the effect. When we talk about the pharmacokinetics of cannabinoids, we must keep in mind the many methods of administration. Research in this area is also challenging because of low concentrations of the substances, rapid metabolism, and distribution by the body, which pose problems separating out the drug.

The fastest route of adsorption is smoking. The drugs in this case are the cannabinoids (THC, CBD, etc.) that the lungs quickly and efficiently deliver to the brain. This method's speed of delivery is comparable to an intravenous (IV) dose. Possibly, smoking's fast-acting delivery increases its abuse potential. The bioavailability (percentage that essentially ends up at the receiving end) of the drugs is affected by multiple parameters of smoking itself. These include the number, duration, and hold-time of the puffs. THC is detected after the first puff of a marijuana cigarette. Peak concentrations are found at approximately nine minutes after smoking. Within two hours without smoking, very low THC levels are detected. An experienced marijuana smoker can titrate their desired effect by increasing or decreasing their lung's tidal volume and hold time. The percentage of THC in a marijuana cigarette is varied by the species of cannabis being used. It is also known that the percentage of CBD (cannabidiol) can modify and lessen the effects of THC. Even though it is theoretically possible, THC does not form from CBD during smoking or metabolizing. Some wonder if the negative effects of the smoke itself outweigh the positive therapeutic possibilities. Lung disease very rarely accompanies marijuana smoking, but common sense should prevail. With maximal effort, the bioavailability of smoked marijuana is about 60%.

Oral administration of cannabinoids has a significantly greater spectrum of variable absorption. The oral route is slower, and it has a lower absorption rate, which results in lower peaks of THC. There are individual variations of absorption and metabolism that are not involved with smoking. The carrier for the oral drug can increase or decrease the availability. At best, an oral dose has an availability of 20-30%. Several other factors are involved in decreasing the dose absorbed from the stomach and liver. The stomach can degrade the drug to a small extent. As the absorbed materials pass though the liver, THC can be metabolized into an active form, 11-OH-THC, and inactive metabolites. This is called the first pass effect. The need for a successful delivery method for oral drugs will be essential if smoking will be replaced as the preferred way to maximize drug percentage. Maximum oral bioavailability occurs after one to two hours. THC can be contained in some liquids as hemp oils are. THC beer shares absorption problems with solid oral presentations.

Because oral administration has poor bioavailability, alternative methods have been developed. The point that can't be missed here is that the separated cannabinoids, such as THC or CBD, may not provide the same major effects alone as if they were together with all the other cannabinoids. Delivery without separation is the goal. The percentage of the major cannabinoids needs to be determined with the rest of the cannabinoids delivered as a whole. Oromucosal (usually under the tongue) delivery gives one distinct advantage: the avoiding of the first pass effect via the liver. For certain situations, the rectal route is available. It also avoids the first pass effect via the liver and has a higher absorption rate than oral. This gives the rectal approach higher bioavailability. Transcutaneous delivery is also an option. It avoids the first pass effect, but the hydrophobic (water-hating) nature of the cannabinoids complicate the absorption process. The aforementioned delivery systems are formulated to basically avoid the side effects of smoking; however, smoking marijuana is much safer than smoking tobacco.

THC blood plasma concentrations decrease very rapidly, which is due in most part to redistribution. This is accomplished by THC's moving to the body's tissues and the metabolizing in the liver. THC is very lipophilic (fat-loving), and it moves to tissues with a high blood flow, such as the lungs, heart, brain, and liver. The deposition is abundant in neutral fat areas of the body and almost absent in the brain. THC's being retained in fat stores indicates it might be conjugated in the fat. This increases stability and enables a prolonged stay. There does not appear to be any toxicity due to this fat accumulation except for possible instances in the epididymal area. This allows deregulation of the cell process, including death of spermatogenic cells.

THC is normally metabolized into 11-OH-THC and THC-COOH. It is interesting to note that the metabolite of THC, 11-OH-THC, crosses into the brain four times faster than THC. Its drug effects are perceived as quicker and clinical effects are markedly psychotropic. 11-OH-THC also leaves the blood faster than THC. This could be due to slightly less protein binding or enhanced crossing of the blood-brain barrier because of the hydroxylated group (OH addition). Originally, the metabolite 11-OH-THC was erroneously thought to be the main psychoactive drug. The effects of 11-OH-THC are significant with edibles because they are created by the liver.

The steady state volume of distribution (Vd) of THC is very large. It is estimated to be 3.4 liters/kg. This is essentially the theoretical volume that would be necessary to contain the total amount of THC at the same concentration as would be observed in the plasma of the blood. Vd's large size indicates most of the THC is in the tissues, instead of plasma. This is somewhat unusual in a drug that is highly protein-bound in the plasma. It is bound around 97-99%.

THC rapidly crosses a placenta. Fetal plasma levels remain less than maternal plasma levels. This crossover of THC is more pronounced in early pregnancy. Breast milk also has detectable levels of THC, which were higher than the maternal plasma level and indicate concentration.

THC is not only broken down in the liver; the brain, intestine, and lungs have the capability and may contribute to the metabolism. It's possible that severe liver dysfunction may not change the amount of THC metabolized.

We have spent the most time referring to the metabolism of THC. This is because the metabolism of CBD is similar. There is oxidation (added OH group) and carboxylic acid

(COOH added). Like THC, CBD has a significant first pass effect in the liver from oral consumption. Contrasting with THC, a significant portion of CBD is excreted unchanged in the feces. CBD can affect the metabolism of THC by slowing the metabolizing of 11-OH-THC into THC-COOH. This could also potentially affect potency. CBD has a low affinity with the CB1 and CB 2 receptors.

What is the process of elimination for THC? Within five days of using THC, approximately 80% is excreted, usually in a metabolized format. This would be either in a hydroxylated or carbolated format. More than 60% is excreted in the feces and about 20% in the urine. The concentration of free THC-COOH and a bound form of THC-COOH enable cannabinoid immunoassays to be performed on urine. The gold standard for measurement of THC-COOH is done by a mass spectrometer/gas chromatograph (GC/MS), not immunoassay. The GC/MS is more accurate with smaller numbers and more specific for each compound being measured. Preparation for using the MS/GC in measurement of THC-COOH usually includes a hydrolysis step that frees the cannabinoids from any conjugates. It depends on how this hydrolysis step is performed, and different methods yield higher results. Keep in mind that if you are taking hemp oils, they may not be pure and can contain enough THC to give you a positive urine test. Reputable manufacturers make this less likely as the product is in a pure form of hemp.

The terminal plasma half-life of THC is very long due to slow release from fat stores and significant enterohepatic circulation. The terminal half-life of the plasma is just over four days; then detectable levels of THC are eliminated from the blood. Detection of THC-COOH is possible even earlier.

True detection of THC in the body (not just the plasma or urine) is very difficult. The fat-loving aspect of THC is mainly responsible for the challenge posed to the lab. Only low concentrations are in bodily fluids. Most of the cannabinoid itself is in the tissues. This includes the hair. Extraction processes are very labor-intensive and complex.

The range and variation of many of these numbers is presented for a very good reason. Let's look at the smoking of just one marijuana cigarette, which has ten grams of THC. Does that transfer into good information for a study? No! You can't easily regulate the size of the puff, the length of time before full inspiration, the time spent in the inhalation phase and the exhalation phase, or wasted burn-time. We want to follow the effect of the THC, and yet we don't even know how much drug was received. The effect of giving a pure form of THC is changed due to the removal of all the other cannabinoids and their effect on the THC. Some studies used immunoassays for identifications and missed some chemicals. Other studies were too short, and valuable information occurred only after the study was stopped.

It is also clear that the blood concentration of THC begins to fall prior to the peak effect in the brain. The blood-brain barrier, which regulates what—and how much—passes into the brain, is also at play. The metabolite of THC, THC-COOH, has a plasma ratio of >1 compared to THC at around forty-five minutes after the last drug use. This can give us some indication of very recent use of THC products; if we could know when the last exposure was, then it might be possible to show cause and effect relationships in regard to an occurrence, in legal terms.

Chapter Three Summary

- The fastest route for absorption of marijuana is smoking; the effects can be felt seconds after the first breath.
- Bioavailability of smoked marijuana is about 60%.
- Oral marijuana's absorption rate varies greatly; it could be one to three hours, with a bioavailability of 20%.
- THC plasma concentrations fall rapidly, which means the brain levels also fall rapidly.
- THC has two basic metabolites: 11-OH-THC and THC-COOH.
- The metabolite 11-OH-THC crosses into the brain quicker than THC, and it may have a stronger effect.
- THC rapidly crosses the placenta.
- Within several hours after using marijuana, the level of THC in the blood is very low; the remaining THC is distributed among fat deposits.
- In a user who chronically intakes high doses, THC can be in the body for weeks.
- Within five days of using marijuana, over 80% of it is excreted; a day or two prior to this, urine levels fall to close to zero, but chronic, heavy users may have a different decay curve.

Chapter Four
Effect of Marijuana on a Fetus and Adolescents

From conception until delivery, a fetus is tied to the mother in many ways. All the things the mother eats, drinks, or smokes can potentially reach and negatively impact the fetus. Marijuana use during pregnancy is somewhere between 3% and 30%. The rates vary as per race, maternal age, and socio-economic status. We are aware that THC crosses the placenta that interacts with the fetus. THC also concentrates in breast milk prior to delivery. We also know that THC can be cleared by the body up to thirty days after exposure to THC. This makes it possible for a fetus to be exposed to THC even if the mother did not smoke marijuana after conception. Metabolites of THC do not cross the placenta.

The amount of THC released from body fat up to 30 days after heavy use is small, especially when compared to the amount released by smoking a joint. THC in the blood that passes through the placenta reaches the fetal brain, and it can potentially remain there for up to four weeks or more if the mother does not stop smoking marijuana. This can cause a little-known effect on development since the endocannabinoid system develops around twelve to fourteen weeks after conception.

Let's look at the endocannabinoid system of a developing fetal brain. Again, the endocannabinoid system is our own intrinsic system that responds to cannabinoids regardless if they come from our own body or external sources, such as marijuana. These receptors are developed in a fetal brain at around twelve to fourteen weeks. The endocannabinoid system (ECS) plays a large role in the brain's connective-patterns; this is critical to how neurons and neural networks process information. The ECS is also involved with cellular signaling. This involved and interactive development in the brain can be disrupted by the outside influence of THC from marijuana. Prenatal marijuana usage can lead to changes in the fetal ECS. These changes include disruption of the position of neurons, changing post synaptic targets, and modifying differentiation of developing nerves fibers, among other things. The exact amount of THC it takes to do this is still unclear. The long-term results of changes brought about by THC exposure are deficits in thought processing and changes in physical, emotional, social, and motor function, all of which carries into adulthood.

In September 2015, the American Journal of Obstetrics and Gynecology published an article entitled "Maternal marijuana use and neonatal morbidity". Over four years, the authors looked at 8,138 women, of which 8.4% used marijuana during pregnancy. The women who used marijuana during the pregnancy were compared to the women who did not. The primary outcomes were related to birthweights less than 2,500 grams, neonatal intensive care unit admissions, five-minute Apgar scores of less than 7, and umbilical artery pH levels of less than 7.10. After adjustments for smoking, other drug use, and race, individual markers for poor outcome were not significantly higher in women who used marijuana when compared to those who did not. This does not contradict what has been discussed about the effects of THC during pregnancy. These effects are consistent and manifest after the baby is born.

In an older research paper, in 1989, Zimmerman et. al discovered that decreased birth weight and head circumference correlated directly with use of marijuana during pregnancy. Again, this does not conflict with the findings in 2015. Both results can coexist. A study conducted by Hurd in 2005 showed that aborted fetuses whose mother had taken large quantities of marijuana during the pregnancy featured developmental abnormalities the fetal growth at mid-gestation. This still can coexist with the 2015 study because the weight-criteria set was 2,500 grams.

At this time, one basic bit of information needs to be clarified. The percentage of THC in today's marijuana is almost three times higher than during the early 1970's. This can make a big difference when comparing studies from after 2000 to earlier studies.

The long-term effects of marijuana use during pregnancy are becoming clearer. Children of mothers who used marijuana during pregnancy are prone to having lower functioning skills, attention deficits, and increased conduct and behavior problems. Several studies have shown the relationship between prenatal marijuana exposure and delinquency.

After birth, prenatal marijuana exposure (PME) affects the sleep-continuity at birth and age three. It also coincides with a higher number of arousals and more time spent awake. Lower composite scores in short-term memory and verbal reasoning were also found at three years of age. At age four, lower scores are found in verbal ability and memory. One study showed no significant differences between the IQs of children during their fix and sixth year and their ninth-through-twelfth years who experienced prenatal marijuana exposure.

As these children got older, the testing changed somewhat when it transferred to more of a neuropsychological format. Using a continuous performance test, children at age six with PME (prenatal marijuana exposure) were more impulsive. At age ten, these children had significantly higher rates of depression and anxiety that directly correlated with PME, attention deficits, hyperactivity, and impulsivity.

Prenatal marijuana exposure (PME) ⟶ double the rate of Delinquency PME ⟶ high anxiety and depression detected by age 10 ⟶ Delinquency

The Child Behavior Checklist (CBCL) was used for many of these research papers on the relationship of PME to delinquency. CBCL is a parent-report questionnaire that rates a child in terms of various behavioral and emotional problems. It measures internalization and externalization. The internal factors measured relate to anxiety, signs of depression, and over-control. The external factors measured relate to aggressive behavior, hyperactivity, and under-control. There are several variations to this checklist. The CBCL has a subtest that assesses delinquency. It has thirteen items that connect lying, stealing, and running away with drug and alcohol use. Prenatal marijuana exposure (PME) correlates with delinquency, but prenatal alcohol and tobacco use does not.

Where in the brain might this take place? It seems as if, considering the information we have, this occurs in the proximal areas of the brain. PME enacts changes in mood, attention, impulsivity, and actual activity. As we discussed earlier, the focus of the endocannabinoid system is in these proximal areas; the PME has changed it.

PME ⟶ change in the endocannabinoid system ⟶ altered mood, attention, impulse control Altered mood, attention, impulse control ⟶ altered behavior

PME is a preventable cause of delinquency. The exact percentage of delinquency caused by PME is unknown, but it is significant. The brain continues to develop until the age of 18-20. It seems as if there is still development of the brain's white matter during the early 20's. Some scientists say it can carry into the 30-40's. Changing patterns in the endocannabinoid system—especially by chemicals such as THC—appear to stop during the early-to-late teens. Let's discuss what we know about teens using marijuana and the changes that occur.

It appears about 30-35% of high school seniors have at least tried marijuana. A Monitoring the Future Survey in 2014 said it was 35.1%. 6% of seniors use marijuana daily. There is an increased risk of impaired performance in school—which begs correlation with decreased IQs—and an increased risk of leaving school early with chronic marijuana use. High school seniors have a significant knowledge deficit about the negative effects of THC on their brain. This includes a lack of knowledge about possible altered-coordination, perception, and balance issues.

A general study conducted by Lorenzetti in 2014 shows there are alterations to the medial temporal, frontal, and cerebellar brain regions with frequent marijuana use. This is a morphological observation; morphology is the study of the form and structure of the brain. Unfortunately, there is very little correlation between these changes and potential psychopathological symptoms or neurocognitive performance. In other words, there is a change in some structures, but there isn't a negative clinical correlation.

Clinical Pharmacology and Therapeutics in June of 2015 had a paper called "Cannabis and the maturing brain". A discussion takes place that should be well-known to—or at least assumed by—those familiar with the effect of THC on a developing brain. The distribution of cannabinoid receptor 1 (CB 1) changes from the fetal development stage to adulthood. There is white matter and grey matter in the brain. Simply put, the grey matter is the core or body of the nerve cell, and the white matter is extraneous. The endocannabinoid system (body's own cannabinoid receptors and cannabinoids) plays a vital role in adolescent brain development. In this adolescent brain, the CB 1 receptors are denser in the white matter than in adulthood. This difference in position and density of the CB 1 receptors allows THC to affect a developing brain more than an adult brain. The levels of the body's own endocannabinoids are also higher during adolescence.

There is a six-fold increase in psychosis with heavy use of THC products by adolescents. This may be mediated by the effect of the THC on the white matter as described above. There are several other possible explanations for this increase in psychosis. The first explanation relates to a genetic connection. If there is a close relative with a psychosis, then THC may accelerate the unmasking of the psychosis. Secondly, THC can adversely affect several other receptor systems such as the serotonin, dopamine, and glutamine systems. These are also affected in a psychosis such as schizophrenia. Of course not all adolescents taking THC products will have a psychosis; this just shows the increased vulnerability.

In the future, the main goal will be to discourage the use of THC products among those with developing brains. This will be in a prenatal sense, or the young adolescent with more CB 1 receptors on their white matter. Dose-related effects are not clearly understood. There might be a dose accumulation effect. It truly is playing with fire. We all need our brain to be at its best.

Chapter Four Summary

- THC crosses the placenta. This can continue to occur up to four weeks after cessation of marijuana usage for chronic, heavy users.
- The endocannabinoid system of a fetus starts to develop at 12-14 weeks, and it can be disrupted by outside cannabinoids such as THC. Cessation of marijuana usage near the time of inception should prevents problems.
- The disrupted endocannabinoid system can lead to modified developing nerve fibers, a change in postsynaptic targets, and a change in their position.
- Children of mothers who used marijuana while pregnant are prone to behavior problems, attention deficit, and lower functioning ability; there is also a higher rate of juvenile delinquency.
- Changing patterns of the endocannabinoid system can occur with THC exposure into the late teens.
- There is an increased risk of decreased school performance in high school for marijuana users. About 6% of high school students are chronic users.
- CB 1 receptors are denser in an adolescent brain than in an adult brain; the THC has a greater chance of changing a developing brain.
- There is a six-fold increase in psychosis among adolescents using high doses of marijuana.
- Developing brains, regardless if they belong to a fetus or an adolescent, should not be exposed to marijuana (except for significant medical exceptions).

Chapter Five
Methods of Getting Cannabis Chemicals
Into Our Body

There are various methods to move the desired chemicals of the cannabis plant from outside the body inside the body. If there is a scientific explanation of a specific method, it will be clarified. Let's begin with the most popular method: smoking a joint.

A rolled-up composite of cannabis called marijuana can easily be smoked. You can roll it yourself with your own paper or buy a rolling- machine for better contour. Very little processing is needed; just light the joint (paper roll) or pipe (marijuana stuffed in the business-end) and smoke it as if it was a regular tobacco cigarette. If this is your first time smoking marijuana, or if this is your first exposure to marijuana in any form, you should take small puffs. The larger the inhale, and the longer you hold your breath, the more exposure to cannabinoids and subsequent absorption of the drugs. The chemicals are absorbed quickly from the lungs, and they go to the bloodstream to be taken to your brain and other areas with cannabinoid receptors. Depending on the percentage of THC present (it would be good to know this), the effect will vary. Again, if this is your first time smoking a joint, start with a very low percentage of THC; a psychotic reaction can result in first-time users who intake too much THC. The range of THC is very wide. If the purchase is made from a reputable (legal) dealer, they will know the concentrations of their plants; they can give you plants with a low percentage of THC (1-3%). Marijuana has a high concentration of tar, roughly four times the levels in regular cigarettes. Illegal marijuana can have many impurities and unknown percentages of THC. Many times with an illegal dealer, there can be other drugs mixed in with the marijuana, which is extremely dangerous.

Notably, there does not appear to be a relationship between smoking marijuana and lung cancer; THC and CBD may have protective qualities. The tar is deposited into your lungs, where it will hang out for quite some time. On the short side, all you need is the joint and a lighter. On the long side, there are many unknown dangers aside from the possibility of jail time associated with the smoking of illegal marijuana.

Alternatives to smoking a joint that still involve smoking are widespread. A glass pipe or a water pipe, called a bong, can be used for different preparations of the cannabis. They can be purchased online or at a neighborhood smoke shop. Hand pipes are small, simple, and easy to use. The smoke is trapped and then inhaled. Water pipes add the water interface, which may or may not add a health benefit; a slightly more complex delivery can be accomplished with a vaporizer. In some states it may be illegal to obtain these unless you are a medical marijuana patient. An added benefit of all methods of smoking cannabis is your ability to stop (self-dosing) when you arrive at the desired effect. All other methods of delivery require a significant delay before the desired effect is reached.

The oral delivery system gives a very wide range of absorption. If the delivery is meant to be absorbed under the tongue (maybe an oil concentrate), then a good percentage of the dose can be quickly delivered to the bloodstream for near-maximal effect. This oromucosal method bypasses the GI tract and avoids the first pass through the liver, which would otherwise metabolize a significant amount of the drug. The first pass through the liver can erase up to 80% of the potential effect. Say, for example, you took an oral dose of 100 milligrams; only 20 mg would arrive in the circulating blood. Tinctures can also be absorbed efficiently when taken under the tongue. Tinctures are a liquid oil that has a concentrated drug. Ingestables are oils that are usually solid. Then, the oil is covered by a capsule and swallowed. Edibles are basically any food with added marijuana. It is important to remember that some cannabinoids can only activated by heat. This limitation explains why edible marijuana is somewhat different therapeutically from smoking. Also, cannabinoids only dissolve in fats and alcohols, so a tea of marijuana does not give any appreciable therapeutic effects.

In Table 1, we see that the equivalency of THC is not just related to milligram-for-milligram comparisons, but several other factors. In the case of edibles, you must factor in the metabolites, which can make the potency significantly higher than expected. It does not necessarily translate into more therapeutic effect, however.

Most people do not like the taste of marijuana, so many recipes have either chocolate or tomato as a base. Marijuana can easily be ground into a powder for incorporation into any recipe. The cannabinoids degrade quickly so making more than necessary is not a good idea. If you are the one eating the marijuana from a recipe, remember it might take over two hours

Inhaled from Marijuana Flower		Edible	
THC in Smokable Flower	100	Edible Package: (100 MG)	100
THC Content	17	Rate of Absorbtion	10
of Content Inhaled	50	THC absorption (mg)	10
of Inhaled Air Exhaled	45	11-0H-THC Conversion	3.5
Gross THC Absorbtion (mg)	22.5	11-0H-THC / THC Equivalent	35.00
Blood Cycle De-Rate Factor	35		
Efffective THC Infusion to Brain (mg)	7.88	Effective THC Infusion to Brain (mg)	45.00

Table 1: Example of Marijuana Equivalency between Inhaled and Ingested Uptake Methods

to be absorbed into the bloodstream, giving an effect. Waiting for the absorption from the first brownie is a good idea before taking a second, and this is partially due to the liver's forming the metabolite 11-OH-THC, which is more potent—and crosses the blood-brain barrier faster—than THC itself. It can give you more effect than you bargained for, and it is called stacking and adding.

The liquid form of marijuana is also somewhat complicated. As a reminder, cannabinoids do not dissolve in water. What are the options? There are two basic ways to get the cannabinoids into a liquid format. The first way is to soak the marijuana in high-proof alcohol (80% or greater) for several days. After you remove the plant, you still have the alcohol, which is a problem with this method. There are many reasons why you might want the cannabinoids, but not the alcohol. Included in these reasons is the possibility it might not mix well with other medications.

This leads us to the second solution for extracting the cannabinoids into a liquid: milk. *Bhang* is the official name for medical marijuana milk. Nonfat milk isn't ideal for this method because cannabinoids like fat. Start by heating a quart of whole milk to a slow boil. Now mix in ¼ ounce of medical marijuana. Lower the heat and let it simmer for about thirty minutes. Pour the liquid through a strainer. If you drink it straight you might find it to be an acquired taste, but it can be used anytime milk is needed.

Using a vaporizer is a format for inhaling concentrated percentages of THC and/or CBD. It requires a special piece of equipment that vaporizes marijuana in its raw form, oils or pellets of concentrate. The amounts available for absorption are unknown. The formation of these concentrated cannabinoid oils is complicated. Special lab equipment is required to maintain a safe environment because isopropyl alcohol, high-pressure CO, or butane are used for the extraction.

Access to 1000's of recipes can be obtained from http:// www.thestonerscookbook.com. "Cannabutter" and making your own cooking oil with marijuana are two favorites. Don't forget that THC is not the only cannabinoid that can be of benefit to you. CBD (cannabidiol) is also in the cannabis plant, and it can be a great source of relief from pain and inflammation. So, even though making all these recipes might be fun, get the right percentages of the right cannabinoid in your mix.

Chapter Five: Summary

- Smoking marijuana is as simple as it gets; you only need a joint and a lighter.
- Bonging or vaporization might decrease some of the negatives of smoking.
- Ingestables (pills) or edibles (brownies) are also alternatives of delivering cannabinoids into the bloodstream.
- Edibles usually include a chocolate or tomato base due to the somewhat unpleasant taste of marijuana; terpenes can decrease the unpleasantness.
- Overdosing on edibles might be more likely due to long absorption-time; this is due to stacking doses. Also, the psychoactive strength can be underestimated because of the metabolite 11-OH-THC, so be aware of the dose of THC per serving.

Chapter Six
Legal Medical Synthetic Cannabinoids
and Illegal Synthetic Marijuana / Spice

There are legal synthetics and illegal synthetics that are very dangerous. The legal synthetics are medications that have a generic name and a trade name; they're not often confused with other medications. The illegal synthetics have many names. They contain an endless combinations of drugs mixed with what is loosely-referred to as synthetic marijuana or spice/K2.

First, let's look at the legal synthetics and what they can do to improve our health. These synthetics are actually cannabinoids that are formed with chemicals in a lab. They exactly match cannabinoids found in marijuana. As we have discussed prior, a single cannabinoid is not as strong or versatile when isolated from all the other cannabinoids. Together, they are synergistic.

Why do we even bother making them if they are not as good? Legally, it was much easier to present a pure form of a drug and get it approved by the FDA (Federal Drug Administration). The first two drugs introduced as synthetic THC were nabilone (Cesamet) and dronabinol (Marinol). Both of these drugs are non-selective CB 1 and CB 2 receptor agonists (stimulators). Initially, these were meant to as a suppressant for chemotherapy-related nausea and appetite-stimulant for AIDS/HIV patients. Marinol and Cesamet are the only synthetic THCs approved in the US. There is also a synthetic analog of the metabolite of THC, 11-OH-THC. It is called ajulemic acid. It has a selectivity for the CB 2 receptor. This gives ajulemic acid significant anti-inflammatory properties. It is being studied for use in cystic fibrosis and systemic sclerosis.

In an effort to use the effects of CB1 receptor stimulation, an anti-obesity drug, which focused on CB 1 receptor inhibition in the brain, was developed. We know that CB 1 receptor stimulation has a role in modulation of food intake, energy, homeostasis, metabolism, and storage. A CB 1 central inhibitor called Acomplia was developed. Weight-loss was accomplished, but there were too many psychiatric side-effects. Interestingly, too much or too little stimulation of CB 1 receptors causes psychiatric side-effects. This is a clear indicator that having our endocannabinoid system in good condition is imperative to many aspects of health and homeostasis.

The research's emphasis switched from central CB 1 receptors in the brain to peripheral CB 1 receptors. This was accomplished by development of medications that do not cross the blood-brain barrier and still manage to block CB 1 receptors. No medications that could be of clinical use have been developed at this time. Medications with CB 2 receptor targets can be of significant use in pain relief, cancer therapy, and any highly-inflammatory disorder. Unfortunately, selective medications that hit CB 2 targets without CB 1 effects have not been developed. This takes us back to using nature's own plant to meet the clinical needs of the patient after modifying the THC/CBD content.

Synthetic Marijuana/ Spice

There are too many names associated with synthetic marijuana to mention, including spice, K2, face weed, mojo, cloud 9, Yucatan fire, skunk, and moon rocks. Spice is promoted as an herbal mixture with several herbs that provides a psychoactive experience similar to marijuana's. The very simple fact is there may be some herbs in the mix, but the psychoactive component comes from a bunch of chemicals. These chemicals make spice very dangerous. It is a situation with unpredictable abuse potential and unpredictable toxicity.

Spice is second only to marijuana on the list of drugs abused by high school seniors. Lack of education about spice leads to the misconception of it as a naturally-occurring substance. Spice is constantly available and easily to access on high school campuses. It is also cheap and undetectable in urine tests. The dangers are greater than with marijuana, and many users have been hospitalized with a bizarre mental picture.

The chemical composition of spice is not well-known because it is not always the same. Some of the original chemicals were moved to Schedule I status (illegal to sell, buy, or use) by the FDA. There were hundreds of synthetic cannabinoids manufactured in the 1960's and 70's. Many of these were subsequently used in spice formations. Chemicals that bind to the CB 1 and CB 2 receptors are used as much as possible. There are phytocannabinoids obtained from non-marijuana plants that can bind to CB 1 and CB 2 receptors. These phytocannabinoids bind at different rates and tenacities than cannabinoids from marijuana. Wild dagga (*Leonotis leonurus*) and Indian warrior (*Pedicularis densiflora*) are two of the more common plants that provide these chemicals. The end result is a very dangerous and highly-variable concentration of psychoactive drugs mixed with some herbals because there is no quality control. The different combinations of these phytocannabinoids are not necessarily meant to be mixed together and can cause a synergistic reaction making them even more toxic.

Synthetic marijuana can be smoked, vaporized, or ingested, too. Over 85% of those who used both spice and marijuana prefer the more constant effects of real marijuana. Others preferred the completely uncontrolled effects of spice. About 80% of spice users are male.

A significant number of health issues can be associated with synthetic marijuana. Rapid heart rates, vomiting, agitation, confusion, hallucinations, and heart attacks have been reported by poison-control centers. Yes, heart attacks have occurred in young spice users. Blood pressure can rise and blood supply to the heart can decrease. Regular spice users can experience withdrawal and addiction symptoms at a much higher rate than with marijuana use.

There have been a significant number of neurological/psychological emergencies caused by the use of spice. Seizure activity, catatonia, and self-mutilation have been reported. Abuse of the cannabinoid receptors can also lead to new psychosis—or unmask old ones. According to a report by JAMA from 2014, 200 people in Colorado go to the ER in one month with an altered mental state after smoking spice.

The Synthetic Drug Abuse Prevention Act was passed in July 2012; its usefulness remains to be proved. It has broad restrictions regarding synthetic cannabinoids. The Journal of the Mississippi State Medical Association has a nice article from May of 2015 called "Top 10 facts you should know. Synthetic cannabinoids: not so nice spice."

Chapter Six: Summary

- There are legal and illegal synthetics. Legal synthetics are cannabinoids formulated in a lab and used for clearly-defined medical purposes. Illegal synthetics can be a number of different dangerous compounds, stolen cannabinoids, or poorly-manufactured fake cannabinoids, such as chemicals.
- Spice is a very dangerous mixture of chemicals; no one can be sure of the effect. There is very little about spice that can be considered natural.
- Spice is the second-most popular illegal drug among high schoolers. The completely unpredictable effects are attractive to some.
- There are two FDA-approved THC synthetics: nabilone and dronabinol.
- ER visits from the use of spice continue to increase.

Chapter Seven
Health Risks Associated with the Use of Marijuana

This chapter is the "no free lunch" portion of the discussion about marijuana. We will take a look at its association with stroke, decreased function of the left ventricle, hyperemesis syndrome, viral loads, changes in pulmonary function, and decreases in cannabinoid receptor binding.

Let's first look at the changes that take place on cannabinoid receptors with chronic marijuana use. There have been some references to mild cognitive dysfunction in chronic marijuana users, but there is no real evidence that this translates to neuropathological changes in the brain. A study highlighted in Neuroscience from 2007 looked at twelve postmortem brains. Six of the brains were from chronic marijuana users and six were from drug-free subjects. None had traumatic brain injuries. All the marijuana users had positive urine tests at autopsy. A decrease in the number of cannabinoid receptors was found with chronic marijuana exposure. THC's binding capacity was decreased, along with CB 1 receptor mRNA levels in some—but not all—areas of the brain. This confused the issue of THC's affecting the receptor protein or the receptor gene. There was a decrease in CB 1 receptors and a decrease in mRNA expression in Ammon's horn (the hippocampus proper). This could be related to memory loss that is suspected to coincide with chronic THC exposure. Overall, there was a decrease in density of receptors and a change in binding capacity and mRNA expression. Our endocannabinoid system is extremely valuable to out body's ability to function. These changes give us pause to consider daily use of marijuana. If it is not absolutely necessary for treatment of a chronic medical condition, then daily use should be avoided. Remember, these subjects were daily users. An October 2015 study by Rigucci in Psychological Medicine showed a change in the corpus callosum of the brain linked to high THC percentages. The corpus callosum is the area of the brain that facilitates interactions between the two hemispheres of the brain. With high doses THC (20%), the connection slowed. This may relate to increased risk of traffic fatalities.

The use of marijuana is loosely connected with increased risk of stroke. There are several articles written about this connection, which we will discuss. The association between use of cannabis and increased risk of stroke is related to approximately a dozen patients who had no other explanation for their stroke. Even though cannabis might have been responsible, the pathophysiology could not be explained. Many were young patients, and most strokes, over 40%, in young patients are drug-related. In several of the reports, symptoms were clearly present almost immediately after using cannabis. This could have been some sort of cerebral vasospasm or vasoconstriction. Several small studies showed lowered blood flow in certain areas of the brain with cannabis. Doppler showed reduced blood flow in the middle cerebral artery during the smoking of cannabis and normal blood flow after stopping. Emboli might be possible because smoking cannabis increases the rate of atrial fibrillation or flutter. With all this said, 15 million people a day smoke cannabis in the US, and yet only a dozen strokes were reported. It does not seem to be a global issue.

HIV/AIDS patients as a group consumes massive quantities of medical marijuana. It has been suggested that the protease inhibitors used to treat HIV were negatively affected by marijuana. This stems from the fact that they are both metabolized by the same system in the liver. Contrary to the hypothesis, the patients who took marijuana had improved immune function when compared to the placebo group, and they gained four pounds during the study. Score one more for marijuana.

If you have heart disease and smoke marijuana, what are the potential problems? An old—but well-done—small study from 1978 looked at left ventricular performance and norepinephrine levels in a few male patients. Both heart rate and ventricular shortening were increased in patients who smoked marijuana, which lasted up to one hour after drug exposure.

Norepinephrine levels did not increase immediately but, at thirty minutes after exposure, they were significantly higher than levels from the placebo group. The level of norepinephrine remained elevated for almost two hours. This is not a good situation for someone with cardiac disease.

Just because smoking is the main method for the use of marijuana, one automatically thinks of negative pulmonary effects. Comparing smoking marijuana to smoking tobacco is somewhat similar to comparing apples and oranges. Two joints per day is considered heavy usage, and yet someone who smokes two tobacco cigarettes per day is a light smoker. They share many chemicals. Tobacco cigarettes cause chronic obstructive pulmonary disease and lung cancer, the leading cause of preventable death. Marijuana smoke causes some mucosal damage in the airways and inflammation. Clinically, there is a cough, phlegm production, and wheezing, as with tobacco smokers. In spite of all this, decreases in pulmonary function and the appearance of lung disease are not clearly present. In a 2012 study from JAMA, the FVC (forced vital capacity) actually increased. This was possibly due to marijuana smokers practicing the deep-breath maneuvers that make their smoking experience more successful. It seems as if an occasional joint, either for pleasure or medical management, would not cause major damage to the pulmonary function of the lungs. Marijuana has four-times the amount of tar in a tobacco cigarette, and yet they share many chemicals; it is difficult to find one case of lung cancer from marijuana, however. The supposition is that the positive effects of joints as a whole is protective. Combining asthma and any smoking does not make sense; it has not been studied for obvious reasons.

Cannabinoid hyperemesis is a real and overlooked syndrome. It occurs in current, heavy users of cannabis. There is a significant amount of abdominal pain associated with emesis. The episodes of severe nausea and unrelenting vomit recur several times. Oddly enough, compulsive bathing occurs; it gives some relief. Medications usually given for nausea and vomiting are not considered useful.

Long term cannabis use ⟶ cyclic episodes of nausea/vomiting ⟶ compulsive bathing ⟶ cannabis hyperemesis syndrome

This can be confused with something called cyclic vomiting syndrome, which is associated with migraines and a possible history of psychiatric illness. If the person is a long-term cannabis user, they need to stop. If we recall our cannabinoid receptors, CB 1 receptors are found in the brain and the intestines system. As large amounts of THC are stored in the fat around the intestine, nausea and vomiting. Nausea and vomiting occurs with stimulation of intestinal CB 1 receptors. Nausea could be stopped by CB 1 receptors in the brain if it weren't for the overpowering massive input from the intestinal CB 1 receptors.

There appears to be a relationship between marijuana use and many acute and chronic mental illnesses. These include bipolar disorder, schizophrenia, psychosis, and depression. Episodes of mania can be triggered in previously-diagnosed bipolar patients. Although marijuana is often taken to waylay anxiety, it might actually intensify ongoing anxiety. Temporary psychotic episodes can manifest themselves, too. If there is a family history with a predisposition for schizophrenia, marijuana use might bring out the symptoms earlier than expected.

What are some of the metabolic effects of marijuana use? In a 2013 article in Diabetes Care, marijuana use was associated with higher (20%) daily caloric intake. Unfortunately, most of these calories were from junk food. Much of this increase in calories was from carbohydrates. THC is stored in fat tissue, and it actually stimulates an increase in the size and number of fat cells deposits. This fat storage change was not true for the liver's fat stores. Insulin sensitivity was only affected in fat deposits, completely unrelated to the metabolism of glucose. In fact, marijuana users have decreased risk of diabetes. This lower incidence was true—even if the person who had used marijuana in the past were not currently using. It is unknown if this is a direct or indirect effect.

The blood pressure of marijuana users is higher than non-users. The increase was variable, but blood pressures were consistently higher. The amount of central nervous system depression found with marijuana is additive with other depressants, such as alcohol or opiates. In the confines of a home, it might not be a problem. In unfamiliar areas, the synesthesia caused by marijuana can be disorienting. Simply put, synesthesia is the stimulation of one sense that then causes stimulation of another sense or thought. These other senses and thoughts can disorient and scare. Thought fragments and impaired memory are also possible.

The increase in ER visits resulting from marijuana use is up to 50% higher in states that have legalized recreational marijuana. These visits were related to panic attacks, high blood pressure, paranoia, and nausea/vomiting. Marijuana accounted for well over 500,000 ER visits in the US last year.

The number of fatal car crashes in the US involving marijuana has tripled. Drugged driving accounts for 28% of traffic-related deaths in 2010. This is 16% higher than it was a decade ago. Marijuana contributed to 12% of crashes in 2010 and 4% in 1999. Alcohol is responsible for 40% of traffic-related fatalities. A driver under the influence of both marijuana and alcohol increases risk of a fatal crash by twenty-four-times (thirteen times with just alcohol).

Illegal synthetic marijuana or spice is excluded from this discussion about the side effects of real marijuana. The exact composition can vary with each batch, which obstructs the showing of cause-and-effect relationships. That said, we know why it is very dangerous; however, an article from April 2015 published by the American Journal of Roentgenology is worth mentioning. In their presentation, they mentioned that synthetic marijuana needed to be added to the differential for an x-ray showing a diffuse micronodular pattern. This pattern is not found with marijuana use, and it is pathological.

Chapter Seven: Summary

- A decrease in the number of cannabinoid receptors—and their binding capacity—in the brain with chronic marijuana use. This could relate to a decrease in cognitive function.
- The corpus callosum shows changes that indicate slower communication between the hemispheres of the brain.
- Stroke, although rare, has been reported with the use of cannabis.
- The protease inhibitors used to treat HIV/AIDS are unaffected by smoking marijuana.
- Both heartrate and the heart's contractility were shown to increase with smoking marijuana. This should be considered if you have heart disease.
- Marijuana has four-times the amount of tar in a regular cigarette, but it does not cause lung cancer. It is hypothesized that the cannabinoids are protective.
- A syndrome called cannabinoid hyperemesis correlates with high levels of THC, and only cessation of use clears it up.
- There are correlations between marijuana use and acute/chronic mental illness.
- Marijuana increases your blood pressure during use.
- The number of fatal car crashes involving only marijuana has tripled over the last decade.

Chapter Eight
Medical Marijuana

This is truly my favorite chapter. You would be hard-pressed to find another substance on earth that has been used as a medicine longer than cannabis/marijuana. Medical marijuana actually focuses on the chemicals in marijuana; in particular, the cannabinoids. Of the many cannabinoids, THC (tetrahydrocannabinol) and CBD (cannabidiol) are the main two. These can be administered by smoking, drinking, eating, or topical/sublingual application. Many of these cannabinoids are synthesized in a laboratory. To truly know about medical marijuana, you must be familiar with the term cannabinoid, especially THC (tetrahydrocannabinol) and CBD (cannabidiol). How they work and how much you need will dictate their benefit. Armed with this knowledge, you can also decrease any potential side-effects.

In separate chapters, marijuana will be discussed at length for its use in cancer care, chronic pain, Alzheimer's, Multiple Sclerosis, and PTSD. This chapter will be a composite of all the areas that marijuana touches medically. Some will have a strong medical basis, and others will have moderate-to-little basis. When possible, the distinction will be made.

The use of cannabinoids for chronic pain started over 4,500 years, and it continues at a high rate to this day. The two main cannabinoids found in marijuana, THC and CBD, have distinct pathways to lessen the impact of pain. If we use the cutoff point of a 50% reduction of pain, many studies did not show a significant reduction. If a 30% reduction in pain was used as the standard, then cannabinoids were successful in the reduction of pain, including neuropathic pain, diabetic polyneuropathy, fibromyalgia, osteoarthritic/musculoskeletal pain, headaches, and cancer pain. The 50% reduction is worth mentioning because many physicians use it as a threshold for determining the success of a procedure.

We can say that THC and CBD have analgesic properties, but not in the usual sense. We know the body has the potential to modulate pain pathways and potentiate the mu (opiate) receptors. THC and CBD can work through—and with—the body's own endocannabinoid system, providing pain relief and sustaining anti-inflammatory action. Together they have more analgesic properties. The body's endocannabinoid system is very active in the modulation of headaches. Reports show marijuana successfully treats migraines. There are clear pathways that explain its success. Even though it is a deep and potentially-unclear subject, it merits a look.

The body's own cannabinoids have been shown to modulate or adjust pain in several ways. They are able to inhibit dilation of blood vessels in the dura, a membrane that surrounds the brain. Endocannabinoids, through CB 1 receptors, can relieve pain of the spinal cord through modulation. There is also evidence that certain genetic variations of the CB 1 receptor cause a predisposition for migraines. The endocannabinoids' usual workload is not being carried out. THC can activate these same receptors. The goal is to dose the THC in a way that minimizes psychotropic effects and maximizes modulation effects. As CBD modulates the effects of THC, it is important to have lower levels of THC and higher levels of CBD. Theoretically, a ratio of 2-4% THC and 4% CBD fits this requirement. The dose and percentages are adjustable for individual needs. Possible explanations for the migraine occurring include a deficiency of endocannabinoids or an overactive metabolism of cannabinoids. A case can be made for trying marijuana with a patient who has migraines that are refractory to traditional medical treatment. Many of the descriptions of how endocannabinoids work in a migraine apply to all types of chronic pain. I have used cannabinoids for my chronic pain for over forty years. When my pain starts to cycle out of control, I use more cannabinoids than usual; maintenance therapy is relegated to a regimen Tylenol/Advil.

The use of joints to treat chemotherapy induced nausea and vomiting, and it has not been well-researched for legal reasons. The oral, synthetic version of THC, dronabinol, has several small studies to support its use for nausea and vomiting caused by chemotherapy. These studies usually compared THC compared to other available anti-nausea medications, and THC showed superior results. Currently, dronabinol is only used for breakthrough nausea. In non-chemo-induced nausea and vomiting, the area affected most by cannabinoids when stopping this reflex might correlate with the same area around the dorsal-vagal complex in the brainstem. In motion-sickness studies, people with higher endocannabinoid levels and higher CB 1 expression had significantly less nausea. The CB 2 receptor's role in nausea is unclear.

Pain relief of rheumatoid arthritis (RA) can't be left off the long list of applications of the manipulation of cannabinoid receptors. In RA, there is continuous inflammation, which begets continuous stimulation of the sympathetic nervous system. This sympathetic stimulation can support the immune system's perpetuation of inflammation. Cannabinoids are known to control the sympathetic nervous system's output and stop inflammation through the CB1, CB 2, and TRP (capsaicin) channels. The CB 1 receptor should be antagonized peripherally with the stimulation of the CB 2 and TRP receptors. This should slow stimulation of the sympathetic system and lower the inflammatory response. All the pieces are in place; but it is still theoretical.

However, the stimulation of appetite by cannabinoids in AIDS/HIV patients is somewhat atypical. The AIDS community notes smoking marijuana leads to less nausea and an increased ability to retain weight; this was not necessarily universal, but it still led AIDS patients to be some of the most prevalent users of marijuana. In a head-to-head study with dronabinol, a synthetic THC and megastrol, a synthetic progesterone, megastrol showed greater weight gain than dronabinol. Whether or not the cannabinoids in marijuana will react negatively to treatment for AIDS by changing patients' metabolisms remains unanswered. This is a point to be considered; but it turns out to be unsubstantiated.

The effects of marijuana on cancers in general will be discussed in a separate chapter, but the effect on one particular cancer, glioma, will be discussed here. In a 2014 article from the University of London, a study with marijuana and mice with a glioma tumor was reported. The mice were given marijuana and then the tumor was irradiated. The tumor was much more susceptible to the radiation than it had been without marijuana. It was thought by the authors that THC and CBD prepared the tumor cells in a pro-apoptotic (ready for death) fashion. Marijuana is known to have pro-apoptotic properties, and it is also known to be anti-metastatic in several tumors.

The endocannabinoid system has modulating effects on cerebral blood-flow. Cannabinoids also alter the rate of glucose-utilization in the brain. In bench-research, high doses of THC significantly decrease cerebral metabolism. CBD was found to have a direct action on isolated arteries, causing dilation. In an animal-model, CBD increased cerebral blood flow in a stroke. Human reports are still at the case-report level. The science behind studying the possible role of CB 1 and CB 2 receptor stimulation—or even inhibition—is fairly clear. CB 1 activation appears to limit the release of glutamate, decrease levels of intracellular calcium, and move toward hypothermia. CB 2 receptor activation within an affected area causes decreased leukocyte adhesion and decreased release of inflammatory side-products. All of these manipulations by CB1 and CB 2 receptors could be applied to stroke-related situations. Again, the ideal dose is unclear, but its intrigue merits additional study.

A large part of the research on applications of medical marijuana focuses on reducing spasticity caused by multiple sclerosis or paraplegia. Multiple different presentations of cannabinoids were used in the studies, including synthetic THC, THC with CBD, and marijuana smoke. An improvement in the modified Ashworth scale for spasticity was used to compare improvements.

There were some improvements, but there were only a few studies overall where overall it was statistically significant. Spasticity is a very complicated issue. The spasms are thought to originate in the area of the brain that controls movement. These are areas with an abundance of cannabinoid receptors. Individually, if you ask an MS patient who

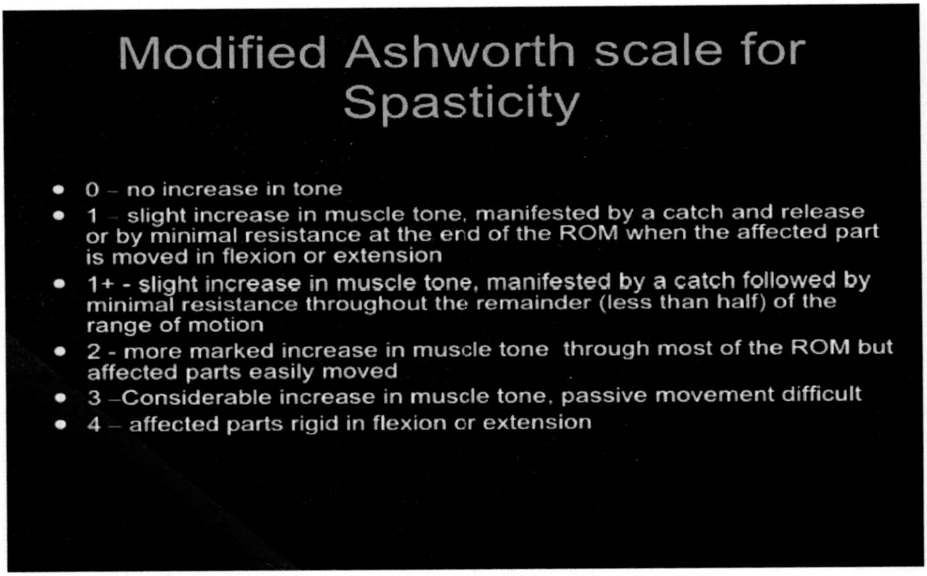

Modified Ashworth scale for Spasticity

- 0 – no increase in tone
- 1 – slight increase in muscle tone, manifested by a catch and release or by minimal resistance at the end of the ROM when the affected part is moved in flexion or extension
- 1+ - slight increase in muscle tone, manifested by a catch followed by minimal resistance throughout the remainder (less than half) of the range of motion
- 2 - more marked increase in muscle tone through most of the ROM but affected parts easily moved
- 3 –Considerable increase in muscle tone, passive movement difficult
- 4 – affected parts rigid in flexion or extension

Figure 5 Modified Ashworth Scale for Spasticity

uses marijuana, a high percentage report marijuana helps significantly.

Surprisingly, marijuana was considered for the treatment of depression. In several small studies, marijuana was compared to a placebo, and there was no difference. Little research exploring this is being done at this time.

It is difficult to say if marijuana relieves anxiety because there are many variables. The factors that need to be looked at are marijuana dose, the timing of the marijuana dose in regards to the anxiety, the type of anxiety, the cannabinoid of focus, and frequency of use. A small study in Neuropsychopharmacology (2011) conducted by Bergamaschi showed cannabidiol (CBD) reduced the anxiety of public speaking. CBD is one of the cannabinoids that has little effect on the CB 1 or CB 2 receptors. Despite this, CBD is known to help regulate systems, and it might be more effective than THC. We know that the endocannabinoid system plays a role in the regulation of anxiety, yet marijuana is known to cause anxiety. All of this has to do with the dose of the cannabinoid, and the specific cannabinoid you are using. In general, lower doses of THC are good for anxiety; higher doses of CBD are good for anxiety, too. There are also variations on the effects of each individual when anxiety is concerned. University of San Paulo, Brazil, in 2011, took anxious patients, gave them a hefty dose of CBD, and then scanned their brains. There was significantly less CBD-activity in areas of the brain that cause anxiety. The concept of marijuana's increasing anxiety can result from self-dosing when you are already anxious and have high levels of endocannabinoids or THC; this might occur with chronic marijuana users. The relief of anxiety from THC can be accomplished if the dose is small and the anxiety is focused on a particular problem (right before a big date or public speaking). General anxiety lacks real focus, so it is not easy to treat with THC at any dose. CBD has no known dose-restriction on relieving anxiety, but one might exist.

The area of sleep disorders has also crossed paths with marijuana. The incidence of sleep disorders is very high in a healthy population at only 20%; let alone those with a chronic illness at 50%. Synthetic THC, CBD, THC-CBD combinations, and marijuana smoke all were studied in an effort to get people to sleep—and keep them asleep. The strongest statement is that cannabinoids may help with sleep disorders. This says cannabinoids are slightly better than placebos. CBD had the edge among the cannabinoids.

Glaucoma and its possible treatment with marijuana is a much debated topic. There really is not much to debate. Glaucoma is a condition where the optic nerve is increasingly damaged over time if untreated. One cause of glaucoma is an increase in pressure around the optic nerve. Medications that lower this pressure are used as treatments. Marijuana or THC have been proven to lower this pressure, too. The problem is the decrease in pressure is short-lived, lasting only for three or four hours. A high dosage of THC leaves many impaired from side-effects because many patients with glaucoma are older. Recently, it has been shown lower blood flow in the area of the optic nerve is also part of the pathology. THC not only lowers the pressure around the nerve, but it also lowers the blood flow and cancels the positive effect.

Tourette's syndrome, a hereditary neuropsychiatric disorder with physical and vocal tics, has been aided by the cannabinoids of marijuana. Even though it is not exactly clear, the cannabinoids are known to help the basal ganglia and hippocampal areas of the brain, which are full of cannabinoid (CB 1) receptors. Using marijuana decreased the frequency of tics, reduced obsessive-compulsive symptoms, and augmented the usual medications for treating Tourette's.

In a study from June 2015 published in The American Journal of Addiction, the use of marijuana to help alleviate the symptoms of opiate withdrawal was basically debunked. Opioid withdrawal scores were the same for users and non-users.

Trials are under way to assess the possibility of using CBD to help treat Ulcerative Colitis, a form of inflammatory bowel disease where ulcers form in the colon. An abstract in Gut from 2015 stated CBD might be beneficial in symptomatic-treatment of Ulcerative colitis.

Initial studies involving animals showed promising implications when using CBD as a neuroprotective agent in settings involving hypoxia. This is from a short cardiac arrest. A study on induced hypoxemia on piglets from 2014 did not show the same promise; the hypoxia was more extreme than prior studies, however. Early work on CBD as an anti-arrhythmic in animals shows promise, but it is too early to move past animal studies.

Childhood seizures refractory to all other anti-seizure medications have been stopped by the use of cannabinoids. This comes from a series of case-reports involving Dravet Syndrome. Research is underway to clarify how helpful it is—and its correct dosing-regimen. CBD and THC can alter the function of the immune system. The effect on the immune system is usually immunosuppressive. This is important, and it may be a new frontier for immunosuppression of autoimmune diseases; possibly, it might even stop graft-rejection.

Chapter Eight: Summary

- This is my favorite chapter.
- Marijuana has been used as a medicine for thousands of years.
- The use of marijuana in chronic pain is extensive. Both THC and CBD are involved with decreasing pain—both neuropathic and osteoarthritic. This deals with modulation of pain and anti-inflammation.
- Marijuana or THC have been used to treat chemotherapy-related nausea and vomiting for many years, usually when the nausea is resistant to other medications.
- Marijuana and THC have been used to increase weight-gain for many conditions, especially AIDS.
- Marijuana has an anti-metastatic property in several tumors.
- Sleep disorders may be helped by low doses of THC.
- Marijuana only helps with glaucoma on a short-term basis.
- CBD may be useful in Ulcerative Colitis.
- Refractory childhood seizures have responded to cannabinoids.

Chapter Nine
Cannabinoids in Immunomodulation and Cancer Treatment with Cannabinoids

There is a significant degree of complexity that surrounds the cannabinoids THC and CBD. If you are going to use marijuana or any of its cannabinoids and desire an understanding of its effects, reading this information is essential. A complete understanding of the presentation is not essential. You will grasp the depth of these cannabinoids' effects, when they enter your body. Then you will have enough respect for marijuana to use it wisely.

There are many areas that pique our interest involving cannabinoids and their respective receptors. Their effects on the immune system and cancer care should be of interest to everyone. The cannabinoid receptor 2 (CB 2) is highlighted here due to its presence on the immune cells of the body. Researchers focused to clarify the function of the CB 2 receptor on these cells in order of occurrence: The B-cells, then macrophages, monocytes, NK cells (natural killer cells), and PMNs (polymorphonuclear). The CB 2 receptors are mostly confined to the blood's immune cells, but they are also found in areas of the nervous system and on neurons. Please refer to Figure 6 for cell types.

Before we go any further, let's just review for a second what all these cells are and what they do. PMN's (neutrophils) and monocytes are white blood cells and are carried in the blood to be ready to fight infections. Monocytes can transform into macrophages in the tissues. Macrophages are assigned to clean up work during an infection. Both neutrophils and monocytes can essentially eat foreign or dead tissue in the body. Monocytes actually have antigens and activate them when necessary. Antigens induce the immune system to produce antibodies. T-cells and B-cells are lymphocytes from the lymph system. They are set up to recognize invaders to the body which could be bacteria, a virus, or fungus (occasionally this all goes wrong and they attack one's own cells). Once an intruder is recognized, the T cells also have different functions. Some of the T-cells send out cytokines, which tell the rest of the immune system what to do. Other T-cells recognize and kill the virus by infecting cells directly or assisting B-cells with making antibodies. Specific antibodies stick to specific cell antigens and kill them. These dead clumps alert other cells in the body to help. Natural killer cells are lymphocytes that can bind to certain tumor and virus-infected cells and kill them by injecting them. Yes, its a very complicated system discussed as simply as possible. Remember these cells have CB 2 receptors and they react to their signals.

The dendritic cell in Figure 6 above shouldn't be confused with the dendrite, which is part of a neuron. The CB 2 receptor is central to the regulation of inflammation and immune functions. CB 2 receptors regulate differentiation between B cells and T cells. They are associated with the balance between T helper cells 1 (Th 1) and T helper cells 2 (Th 2). Th 1 cells are pro-inflammatory and Th 2 cells are anti-inflammatory. CB 2 receptors also suppress macrophages from multiplying

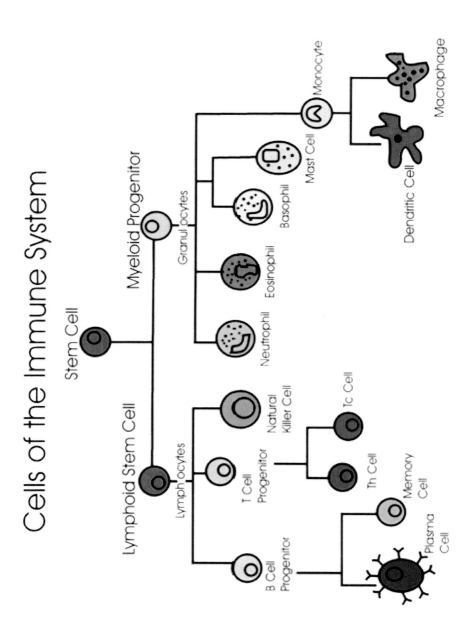

Figure 6 Cells of the Immune System

and releasing pro-inflammatory substances. In the neutrophil, migration is suppressed. In contrast, the killer T cell is signaled to migrate.

The activity of the CB 2 receptor may depend on the state of the target cell population and vascular cells at the site of the infection. Can all these changes, which are caused by CB 2 receptor modulation of the immune systems cells, lead to reduced resistance to infections? A study by Molina from 2015 looked at the effect of THC on primates with simian immunodeficiency virus. THC exposure (CB2 stimulation) reduced viral load, replication, and inflammation. At the same time, further disease progression was slowed. However, appearances are deceiving; the effects of CB 2 receptor stimulation need to be incorporated into a real-life situation where the body is under attack, such as infection or cancer.

We spoke earlier about the negative effects of THC exposure on adolescents. Moretti, in the J of Neuroimmune Pharmacology (2015), proposed that if the adolescent brain is exposed to THC during development, then it's possible that the anti-inflammatory action during development can became pro-inflammatory later in life. This pro-inflammatory situation may send these individuals on a pathway to immune and neuro-inflammatory diseases. The concern of using marijuana during cognitive development is the risk of paying a price for it later in life. This is thought provoking and concerning at the very least.

The anti-inflammatory action of the stimulated CB 2 receptor is unique. It does not mimic NSAIDS or aspirin. It has no known effect on coagulation. A substantial number of diseases can be help by manipulation to produce a desired outcome. These include—but are not limited to—multiple sclerosis, rheumatoid arthritis, IBD (inflammatory bowel disease), modulation of post-stroke ischemic injury, spinal cord injury, and more.

The immune system of the brain is slightly different than the rest of the body. Microglia are the resident immune cells of the brain. These microglia can differentiate into macrophages if stimulated by a perceived threat. Peripheral monocytes normally can't penetrate the blood-brain barrier. The brain relies on the flexible microglia cells. The mediators of peripheral-inflammation can also be present in the brain, possibly leading to neurodegenerative diseases (active inflammatory process). Activated microglia cells may be the cause behind continuous inflammation. If activated by chemicals, including THC, CB 2 receptors on the microglia can slow the process. The two sides of the microglial cell are neuroprotective and potentially neurotoxic.

Immunomodulation (altering or adjusting of the immune system) can change the treatment of Parkinson's, Alzheimer's, ALS, Huntington's, and more. Cannabinoids, as we have mentioned, direct affect immune cells. The effects do not end there; these effects continue to alter the expression of chemokines and cytokines, which are involved in a network of signaling among immune cells. This follows with a continuous role in maintaining balance between pro-inflammation and anti-inflammation. As mentioned prior, it has been difficult to produce compounds that are pure CB 2 agonists. The compounds not only stimulate CB 2 receptors, but also, usually in a dose-related fashion, stimulate other receptors and change the effects. This holds especially true for THC because it also stimulates CB 1 receptors.

There is a thin line between sustaining a well-balanced immune system and using medications to help us return it to a normal state. We could actually make things worse by using incorrect doses or unknowingly stimulate receptors other than CB 2 receptors. Cannabinoids appear to be potentially great tools; we need more information and research to maximize this potential.

Cancer Treatment with Cannabinoids

The complex role of cannabinoids in cancer treatment—not just symptom relief—needs clarification. There is evidence from cell-culture systems and animal models that THC and other cannabinoids may inhibit the growth of some tumors. I emphasize that this is in cell-culture systems and laboratory animals. This appears to occur by changing signals that lead to the arrest of growth following cell death. In culture systems, THC and CBD have shown anti-proliferative effects on several different tumor cells. The list of the types of tumor cells where cannabinoids appear to have this anti-proliferative effect is long and varied. Growth-inhibition in animals has been shown in gliomas, thyroid epitheliomas, leukemia, neuroblastoma, skin cancer, breast cancer, colorectal cancer, and many more. The presence of CB 1 and CB 2 receptors is necessary for this anti-tumor effect.

There are several mechanisms proposed for the anti-tumor effects. Most of these possibilities involve direct access to the cell by stimulation of the CB 2 receptors. This will directly affect induced cell death, inhibition of cell growth, inhibition of cell angiogenesis (formation of new blood vessels), and metastasis. In some animal studies, cannabinoid administration changed the normally-hyperplastic vascular system of a tumor into a small, differentiated, and impermeable system unable to sustain angiogenesis. Without angiogenesis, tumor can't grow.

Cannabinoids are not always used alone in the treatment of a cancer. Sometimes they are combined with other agents to work against the tumor from several different pathways. This synergistic approach has been used in multiple animal models with some success. The usual cannabinoids are THC that is combined with CBD. This combination allows less THC to be used while maintaining anti-tumor effectiveness. This is especially true for the anti-glioma effects.

Can we use THC/CBD in human tumors and human studies? The lack of human studies is a dismal disappointment. From what we learned above, it would seem we were well on our way to a success story. The disappointment is not in the failure to get good results; rather, there are no real studies. There are numerous anecdotal reports of people taking cannabinoids and curing their cancer. Most of these were from people who also underwent standard therapy. I have discussed the use of marijuana with many patients in my medical practice. In their minds, marijuana was integral to their care. I would be hard-pressed to avoid cannabinoids during standard therapy if I had cancer. Of course, this is backed up by many animal studies and knowledge of how cannabinoids work. The changes, if they occur in a legal atmosphere surrounding marijuana, may prompt human research. The work must start from the beginning phases of research. How do the cannabinoids need to be delivered? Which cannabinoids should be used? Smoking cannabinoids gives the full effect because they all work together. Should we just smoke them? Our legal system, the medical system, and researchers have let us down on this topic. The public has somewhat taken it into their own hands through legislation to clear the use of marijuana. Can we recover and do some valuable research? Why has so much time been spent on animal studies? It's not as if cannabinoids and marijuana were never used by humans for millennia. The recreational and medical use of marijuana increases. If animal studies are excluded, the positive effects on tumor treatment appear even less impressive. Animal studies were all that researchers could legally carry out. High doses of cannabinoids may actually result in an effect opposite anti-cancer efforts. Several research scientists are concerned that many of the mediums for cell tissue research were carried out in an environment that did not resemble the environment inside a living body, where cells are hypoxic and acidic. Could this drastically change the results? Maybe, maybe not; we need to know.

What if the research started by combining traditional cancer treatment and cannabinoids? Simple, yes? No, it would not be simple. The agents used to treat cancers are very toxic to the human body. CBD in small concentrations inhibits several drug-metabolic enzymes. This can increase toxicity and change the performance of the cancer drugs. In 2014, a study by Mol. Cancer Ther. showed a combination of THC/CBD, and the radiation was synergistic against a glioma. Again, this was an animal study, but it was designed to answer some questions, possibly enabling human study. This was a study that did not use chemotherapy medications, so the metabolism question is moot. Some of this data can be collected retrospectively since many cancer patients on chemotherapy used marijuana. Did the survival rate change? We should have this information; was it documented incorrectly?

Some of the conflicting data focuses on the number of CB receptors present on a tumor. A high, expressed number of CB receptors can be a good or bad prognostic sign. In pancreatic, squamous cells and prostate cancers, numerous CB receptor are associated with a poor prognosis. In hepatocellular cancer, numerous CB receptor can be a plus. Treatment may entail checking numbers of CB receptors and assuring there are enough to make a difference.

Chapter Nine: Summary

- Cell tissue and animal studies indicate we may have a unique opportunity to use cannabinoids in cancer treatment via combination with current treatments.
- In the treatment of a glioma, two methods of using cannabinoids appeared to help either orally or through direct injection into the tumor—in animals
- We need drug-interaction studies—cannabinoids' interaction with chemotherapy agents.
- A discussion about the use of cannabinoids in cancer care should be had between the treating physician and the patient; they may both learn.
- Researchers need the tools to carry on the needed studies and enable a full-assessment of cannabinoids in cancer; remove the legal concerns related to using cannabinoids in research and fund the research.
- Knowledge of marijuana and its cannabinoids will lead to the respect it deserves as an amazing herb.
- Cannabinoids' ability to decrease inflammation in the brain is a scientific probability; further clarification on dosing and methods of delivery is necessary.

Chapter Ten
Use of Marijuana / Cannabinoids in Multiple Sclerosis

Multiple Sclerosis (MS) is an autoimmune disease. This means a person's body has turned against itself. This is an immune-system malfunction that causes your body to perceive your own cells as the enemy. MS is also a progressive disease without a known cure. Comprehensive care can be directed toward symptom-management and strategies to slow the progress of the disease. The nerves of the brain, brain stem, and spinal cord, are inflamed. The specific activity is the destruction of the protective coating around a nerve called the myelin sheath. This process occurs over a variable period of time, and the nerve cells lose their ability to transmit impulses. The symptoms are extremely varied. Fatigue, depression, dizziness, blindness, incontinence, and loss of certain voluntary muscle control is usually followed by spasticity. Over 90% of MS patients have some form of spasticity. This spasticity is usually found intermittently in the legs, and it can be extremely painful. The sclerosis (scarring) shows the brain/spinal cord's condition after nerves and myelin are lost.

There are over a dozen disease-modifying drugs currently approved by the FDA for MS. The usual medications used to waylay the symptoms of spasticity from MS are Baclofen and Zanaflex. Both medications can relieve some of the spasticity and spasms, but the relief is varied and sometimes absent. Not only are these drugs only partially successful at relief of spasms; they are also sedatives that can cause muscle-weakness. This is not a very reassuring remedy.

We have talked about cannabinoids, their potential in co-ordinating muscle effort, and their anti-inflammatory properties. As of late, there has been a variable explosion of chatter about using cannabinoids in the field of neurology, particularly for neurological disorders including MS. I say chatter because most of it is not backed by any science. Sativex, which is a combination of THC (tetrahydrocannabinol) and CBD (cannabidiol), has been approved in Canada for reducing the spasticity symptoms of MS. Let's take a look at what we know;

Sativex is a combination of THC and CBD in a near-equal ratio of 1:1. It is dispensed in an oral mucosal spray in order to avoid any first-pass metabolism in the GI tract. THC and CBD appear to work synergistically against the spasticity of MS. THC has its role in the stimulation of the cannabinoid receptors, and CBD is an anti-inflammatory, which helps to modify the negative effects of THC (especially the psychoactive effects).

When spasticity and subsequent treatments thereof are measured for success, the H/M ratio can give a simple and somewhat precise measurement. This is simply a ratio between the Hoffman-reflex and muscle response (see Figure 7). The M response is the response of a muscle recorded on an EMG to the stimulation of a nerve. The H reflex is a reflex test that verifies the presence or absence of problems in the corticospinal tract. It can be measured in several areas of the body. The corticospinal-tract's neurons are what are called the upper motor neurons.

They have more control of muscular function, and they are not directly involved with muscular innervation. The H reflex is usually increased in a spastic lower limb, while the M response is unaffected. Having a rudimentary understanding of the H/M ratio is necessary to understand many of the studies done on multiple sclerosis. The H/M ratio can determine if a treatment is a success or failure. The H reflex can be positive in many different neurological conditions including MS, ALS, and spinal cord compression. Figure 7 gives a visual of the H/M ratio.

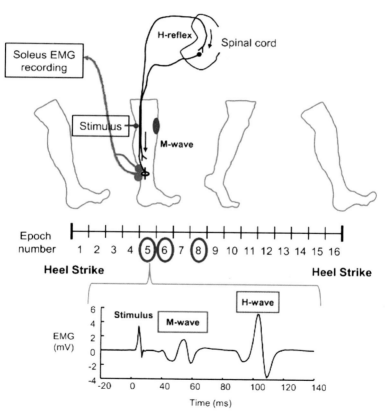

Figure 7 H / M Ratio

A great article in the J Neurol. from August 2015 looked at the effect of Sativex on the H/M ratio and corticospinal-excitability in patients with progressive multiple sclerosis. It was double-blinded and placebo-controlled, and it had a crossover (patients on both sides of the research). This is solid research with a definitive outcome. The outcome was not as expected, neurophysiologically, but it met clinical expectations. The H/M ratio did not improve significantly, but the patients showed more than a 20% improvement on the Ashworth-scale (Figure 5) with Sativex. The authors concluded that the efficacy of Sativex continues to be positive in the treatment of spasticity from MS, but the cause of the spasticity, which was once certain, is now in question. This points toward other spinal and/or supraspinal mechanisms as possibly being responsible for the spasticity due to the lack of changes in the corticospinal-excitability (lack of H/M ratio improvement). Of course it's difficult to treat a symptom if we are unsure of the origin.

The general use of marijuana (smoked or otherwise) is not as positive as the two components used above: THC and CBD. This is contrary to usual findings with marijuana and cannabinoids. Some of the spasticity seemed to improve (unmeasured), but posture and subsequent balance were impaired, along with cognition. People without MS also have impaired balance and cognition, but the MS in addition to marijuana exacerbated the imbalance. It is always difficult to separate out the euphoria and pain relief of marijuana from the perception of decreased spasticity. If we are to interpolate the way THC and CBD were used in the J Neurol study, then we want the marijuana to have a low THC content and high levels of CBD. A sample with 1-4% THC and 4% CBD resembles ideal doses (personal conjecture, not research).

Several studies with patients with MS showed decreased cognition when marijuana was used. A study in Neurology in 2011 showed significantly lower scores on processing speed, working memory, and executive functions in MS patients who used marijuana. They were all regular users, and only twelve hours transpired between cessation of marijuana use and testing. Let's look at this; as far as memory goes, marijuana does not wipeout existing memories. The change in memories involves short-term memory its subsequent move to long-term memory.

We know our own endocannabinoids work on memory-formation, so the story is not as simple as it appears. Low doses of marijuana have shown negligible effects on memory loss. Waiting twelve hours to measure short-term memory in a chronic user does not produce valuable information. The leach-period for chronic users probably ranges from two weeks to a month. Small studies have shown the return of normal short-term memory after cessation of marijuana.

Why Use Marijuana or Products of Marijuana in MS?
- Reliable research shows that cannabinoids (in particular Sativex) can improve the spasticity from MS.
- Improvements occur in pain-scores, night-spasms, and sleep-quality.
- CBD is a different kind of anti-inflammatory, and it may, over a long term, affect relapses.

Why Not Use Marijuana or Marijuana Products?
- Short term memory is affected (dose effect is involved).
- Balance and posture worsen.

Reasons against using marijuana or marijuana products may be dose-related, especially for THC. A low dose of THC and a high dose of CBD should be considered if you decide to use; CBD is protective against many of the negative side effects of THC, and it does not negate positive effects. It may decrease the relapse rate, however.

Why are there only a few animal trials involving MS? Mimicry of spasticity from MS during Animal trials is impossible, which makes it difficult to show possible success of using marijuana to relief the symptoms of MS. This also complicates attempts to clarify the specific areas responsible for the spasticity.

Chapter Ten: Summary

- Sativex is approved in Europe and Canada for MS spasticity. It is a combination of THC and CBD. It is given in an oromucosal mixture and works synergistically against the spasticity

- The H/M ratio can give us reliable information as to the success of an anti-spasticity treatment (most of the time).

- Sativex improved spasticity, but did not improve the H/M ratio. The origin of the spasticity is now in question

- There is a question of increased loss of balance with marijuana, along with decreased cognition in MS patients.

- It is difficult to mimic the spasms of MS in animal studies

- CBD may lower relapse rates

Chapter Eleven
Marijuana in Neurological Disorders:
Seizures, Parkinson's, and Alzheimer's

What are the molecular targets of the cannabinoids used in the treatment of neurological disorders? We are well aware by now that THC (tetrahydrocannabinol) is associated with the cannabinoid receptors CB1 and CB 2. This relationship is quite clear, and it can be proven clinically and in the lab. The concentration of cannabinoid receptors is high in important areas behind several neurologic diseases. CBD (cannabidiol) has a significant effect on neurological diseases; which receptors it actually interacts with to give these effects is unclear. We know that CBD does not usually interact with CB 1 and CB 2 receptors except at super high doses. So, it is unlikely that CBDs assist with the treatment of neurological disorders through the endocannabinoid system. The proposed target of CBD was described in Neurotherapeutics, August 2015. These molecular targets are associated with intracellular calcium levels in a regulatory fashion. In animal studies, there appears to be age-related and disease-related changes to the endocannabinoid system in neurodegenerative diseases. Taking advantage of the capacity for cannabinoids to work together and synergistically increase their positive effects is imperative for neurodegenerative diseases. The range of positive effects include decreases in motor symptoms and neuroprotection. Let's now look at how cannabinoids can help several of these neurodegenerative diseases.

Parkinson's disease is by definition a loss of dopaminergic neurons in the substantia nigra (midbrain, part of the basal ganglia). For the person with Parkinson's, it is a chronic, progressive disorder. The primary motor symptoms associated with Parkinson's are a resting tremor, "slow" movements with a reduction in spontaneous movements (bradykinesis), rigidity (muscles remain in more of a contracted format), and postural instability (loss of reflexes to maintain upright posture). Secondary motor symptoms are a frozen or stuck gait; imagine your feet are stuck to the floor and initiating the first step is difficult. Repetitive actions are difficult. Swallowing is reduced and drooling occurs. Affected non-motor functions include a loss of smell, mood disorders, low BP when standing, fatigue, anxiety, and many more. Essentially, nothing works the way it used to—or should. It is the second-most common neurodegenerative disease (second to Alzheimer's).

Evidence shows modulation of signals from the basal ganglia is a prominent component of the endocannabinoid system (Figure 3). The basal ganglia are a complex network of neurons that coordinate activity involved with movement from different regions. Dysfunction of one or more of the components of the basal ganglia results in diseases that unmask involuntary movements or show difficulty initiating or terminating movements. The endocannabinoids are highly concentrated here, as are exchange signals coming and going from the dopaminergic, glutamatergic, and GABAergic signaling systems. The endocannabinoid system undergoes changes related to Parkinson's. This explains some of the motor inhibition seen in Parkinson's. The substantia nigra (problem area for Parkinson's) has the highest density of CB 1 receptors and the highest levels of endocannabinoids. Figure 8 gives a clear visual of the area affected by Parkinson's and the specific changes that occur. This visual is from the Blausen, gallery C, 2014 collection.

Cannabinoids have an aspect of neuroprotection. They can reduce oxidative injury, excitotoxicity, and calcium influx. Excitotoxicity is the pathological process that damages nerve cells with excessive stimulation by neurotransmitters. In an experimental model of Parkinson's, cannabinoids decreased an already-increased oxidative level of stress and increased the density of CB 2 receptors. The reduction of the oxidative stress was unrelated to cannabinoid receptors.

Oxidative stress is an imbalance in the body by increased presence of free radicals. A free radical is an oxygen molecule that has at least one unpaired electron. This unpaired electron is unstable. It will combine with DNA, proteins, or lipids, and it will destabilize the cell components. Increasing the body's ability to remove these is always a good idea.

There is strong rationale for thinking cannabinoids can help with Parkinson's. First, the presence of some of the largest concentrations of CB 1 and CB 2 receptors in the body is in the area of the neurodegeneration with Parkinson's. Second, the endocannabinoids are involved in fine-tuning motor movements with dopaminergic receptors. Third, changes occur in Parkinson's that affect the endocannabinoid system, suggesting replacement cannabinoids may be necessary.

There is bench-evidence that endocannabinoids and cannabinoid agonists can decrease the re-uptake of dopamine with decreased transport away from neurons. This gives a plau-

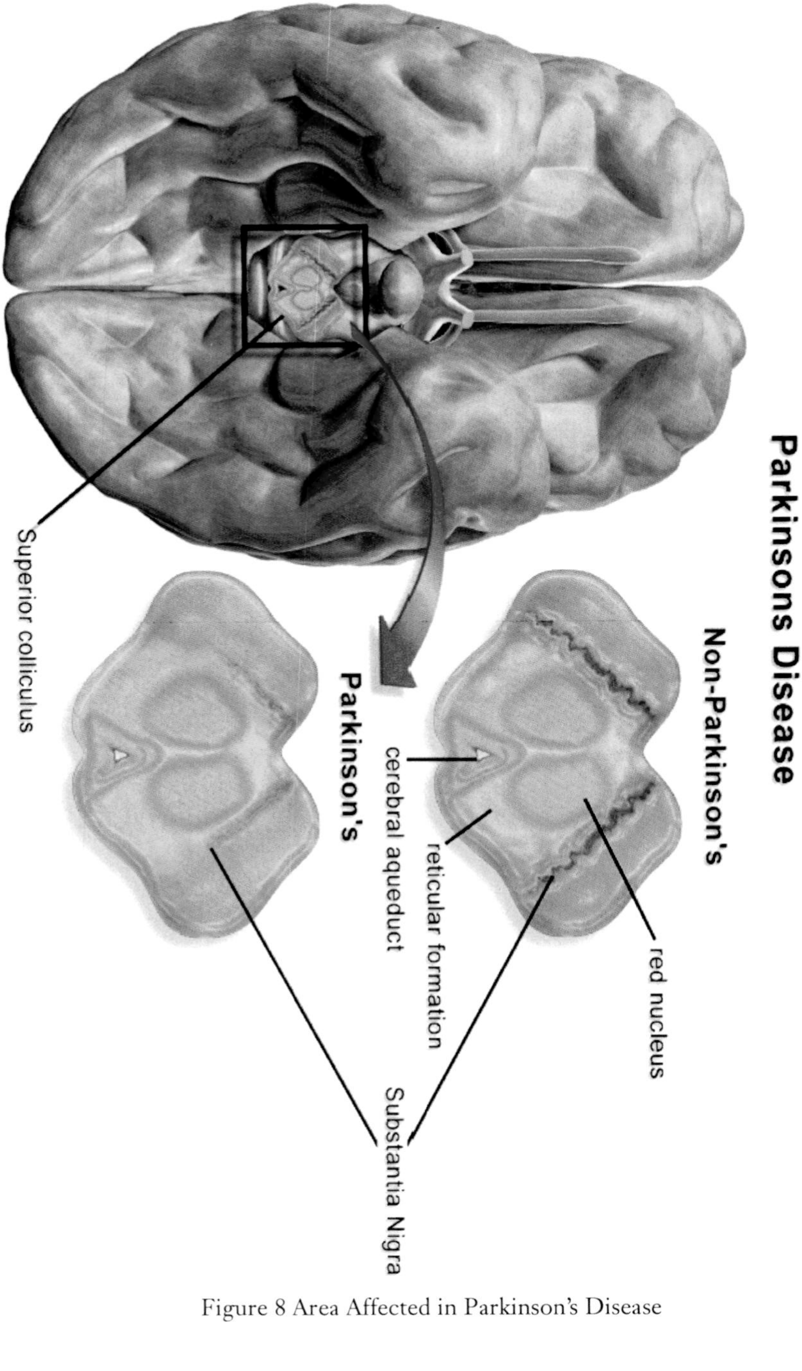

Figure 8 Area Affected in Parkinson's Disease

sible reason to look at cannabinoids in a system with depleted dopamine such as Parkinson's. This potential could help fine-tune neural networks and decrease the dyskinesia (involuntary muscle movements). The clinical trials using CB 1 receptor agonists did not show any relief from dyskinetic symptoms. There was also conflicting data, which essentially pointed toward other receptors. Albeit convoluted, the CB 1 receptor needed antagonism, and the neurological system needed cannabinoids to modulate and adapt functioning at non-cannabinoid sites. The symptomatic stages of Parkinson's showed significant up-regulation of CB 1 receptors, which effectively decreased motor activity. This may explain the effectiveness of antagonist for CB 1 receptors.

CB 1 and CB 2 receptors are induced in response to brain damage and inflammation. Several different bench-models have shown CB 2 receptors in glial cells (non-neuronal, homeostatic cells in the brain) and on neurons themselves to provide neurological protection. Several minor bench-models showed activation of CB 2 receptor to protect against an ischemic insult.

The Summary For Parkinson's And The Use Of Cannabinoids In Humans Is:

- Demise of dopaminergic cells leads to neuroinflammation, in part by glial cells increased CB 2 activation; shelters dopaminergic cells from inflammation and may modulate microglial cell activity.
- There is a significant amount of theory about the possibilities in humans. It is difficult to give a pure CB 2 agonist because it does not yet exist for humans. A small study with motor tests evaluating Parkinson's patients who smoked marijuana showed significant improvement in tremor,

rigidity, and bradykinesis. This work was presented in the March 2014 Clin. Neuropharm. Work is in progress on several other human trials.

- CBD dose leads to less microglial migration, which leads to less pro-inflammatory mediators.
- There is a work-in-progress involving humans. There is not enough information to proceed to large-scale trials. A small study in the J of Psychopharmacology Sept 2014 showed CBD improved well-being and quality-of-life scores in Parkinson's patients.

THC should rarely be used alone in neurodegenerative disease treatment. At the very least, CBD should be included if marijuana itself is not. These cannabinoids are synergistic. CBD can be used alone, but it is probably also synergist when added to THC. We cannot conclude that marijuana, as a whole, is not the best format. It should be included in all head-to-head testing.

Alzheimer's disease is the most-common neurodegenerative disease and the primary cause of dementia. It is a progressive disease without known treatment. After their symptoms become apparent, Alzheimer's patients live an average of eight years. It is unclear if Alzheimer's always starts in the exact same area of the brain; but some of the pathology is similar in all Alzheimer's patients. Plaques and tangles are terms used to describe this pathology. Plaques are protein fragments that are deposited and built-up between nerve cells. Tangles are other proteins that build-up inside cells. These start to build-up in areas of the brain responsible for memory, and then they spread. In late stages of Alzheimer's, patients lose the ability to have a conversation—or even respond to their environment. Mood and behavior problems can be substantial with aggression and agitation. Agitation and aggression are a nightmare for caretakers. According to the Alzheimer's Association, one out of nine Americans over the age of sixty-five have Alzheimer's. Currently, about 5.5 million Americans have this disease.

Cannabinoids' ability to modify behavior, modulate neuroinflammation, and stop oxidative stress makes them attractive for the care of Alzheimer's patients. The current medications that treat some of the negative behavior of Alzheimer's have some serious side-effects, and they are not always successful; this includes the atypical antipsychotics.

The success of cannabinoids in treatment of neurodegenerative diseases, albeit limited, makes them attractive as potential adjunctive therapies for Alzheimer's patients. CB1 and CB 2 receptors are particularly interesting; the wide distribution of CB 1 receptors in the memory centers, especially the cerebral cortex and hippocampus, makes them a key target. CB 2 receptors' anti-inflammatory action and ability to induce removal of protein plaques from human tissues (Brain Res. 2009) is another focus.

A 2015 study in CNS Drugs looked at numerous studies to determine if there was an answer to the question about cannabinoids' role in the treatment of Alzheimer's. The focus was on studies that dealt with the use of any cannabinoids. There was a paltry number of studies and only sixty-seven total participants. It appears most of the patients had a positive effect from the cannabinoids. In these studies, the cannabinoid was a synthetic THC for the most part. Forty hospital patients were given synthetic THC in a 2014 study from the Am J Geriatr. Psychiatry. Motor agitation and aggressiveness decreased significantly. The intensity of research should be far greater because most feedback from numerous studies were positive and there over 5 million patients with Alzheimer's. If the side effects are not enough to discontinue the cannabinoids and each of these 5 million Alzheimer's patients has at least one caregiver who needs help, then why are they not getting help? Is it just because the help would come from marijuana? At this point in their life, the Alzheimer's patient deserves the dignity cannabinoids may give. The focus is not on the caregiver; it is on ensuring there are caregivers.

What about Marijuana and Alzheimer's?

Seemingly, there are some answers to the treatment of Alzheimer's agitation and aggression that we are ignoring for the most part. Maybe our lawmakers do not have any family members with Alzheimer's. Here, even more so than in many other areas, marijuana can help. Marijuana is not a Schedule I drug. Call your members of Congress and the FDA and get them moving toward a change of classification for marijuana. There are many tweaks that can be instituted to solidly reclassify it as an herb. For example, I see no evidence that we need a plant with levels of THC at 15-20%, levels currently common among plants. 4% fits criteria for medical marijuana. For recreational purposes, 4% was enough in the 60's and 70's. Researchers need access to marijuana, as do patients with medical needs. Marijuana can possibly be reclassified as a general herb with restrictions. These restrictions would include age (voided if there is a specific medical need), percentage of THC (less than 10%), etc. Again, inundate your lawmakers and the FDA with requests for the reclassification of marijuana according to its herbal origins. My apologies for this digression; obviously, this is an emotional area. It is fully discussed in Chapter 14.

The area of seizures, particularly children's seizures, and marijuana, lacks research—but not emotion. Families have had to move to states where medical marijuana was legal to get the only treatment that helped their children's seizures, CBD-enriched cannabis. Some states had refused to give the CBD-enriched cannabis orphan-drug status. This seizure disorder is usually Dravet syndrome, which is an intractable form of epilepsy that begins in infancy. These children have several types of seizures; potentially hundreds per month. In a generalized reporting system from parents of these children, over 80% had less seizures and other symptoms were improved, including mood and sleep, with cannabis products. The usual treatment was a high concentration of CBD or a ratio of low concentrations of THC and high concentrations of CBD called Charlotte's Web. These are the same concentrations necessary for almost all medical marijuana research. The American Epilepsy Society and the Dravet Syndrome Foundation both have a party line: there is not enough research and the risk-benefit ratio does not support the use of cannabis. If the best current medications are not controlling the seizures from any viewpoint, how is trying a cannabis extract a bad idea? I can get back on my soapbox again, but I will hold off while we look at how cannabis helps with seizures.

We have biological (not necessarily human) data that clearly shows CBD and THC have anti-seizure properties. Many of these studies were done twenty-thirty years ago. THC has anti-seizure properties because of CB 1 receptors, which is only true at low doses. CBD, which does not work at the cannabinoid receptors, may work through its anti-inflammatory effects. Initial data from a study being done by Devinsky in 2014 showed Epidiolex (cannabidiol purified at 98%) reduced seizures in medically-resistant epilepsy by a median of 32% with three out of nine Dravet patients experiencing no seizures. This study was uncontrolled and unblended; possibly, it should be repeated with controls. None of these studies showed significant side-effects when compared to the side-effects of traditional medical treatment. Lack of side-effects was particularly true with CBD alone. Why shouldn't you try CBD if there are no side-effects and the seizures are intractable?

Most of these patients are children. We have discussed the potential harm of marijuana on the developing brain. Having up to 300 seizures in a week is also significantly negative for a developing brain. There are possible drug interactions in the area of metabolism. The primary neurologist should definitely know if the patient takes a cannabinoid and watch for changing levels of non-cannabinoid drugs. If you stick with a CBD concentrate and eliminate THC from the equation, the risk-benefit ratio of using a cannabinoid seems promising. Further research will clarify many aspects. Until then, cannabidiol (CBD) may treat resistant epilepsy.

Chapter Eleven: Summary

- The concentration of cannabinoid receptors is very high in many neurological disorders.
- CBD has a significantly positive effect on some neurological disorders; this may be achieved through the novel cannabinoid receptors, not CB 1 or CB 2.
- Cannabinoids can reduce oxidative injury, excitotoxicity, and calcium influx.
- There is solid rationale and good bench-work for using cannabinoids for Parkinson's.
- CBD improved well-being and quality-of-life scores in Parkinson's patients.
- THC should not be used alone in neurodegenerative diseases; CBD should be included.
- Activation of CB 2 receptors can help remove protein plaques in Alzheimer's.
- Cannabinoids can decrease the aggression and agitation of Alzheimer's.
- Children with Dravet syndrome evidence cannabinoids' ability to control uncontrollable seizures.

Chapter Twelve
Marijuana in Chronic Pain and How to Use it

The use of marijuana and its components for the treatment and relief of pain spans over 4,500 years. There are around 30 million people with chronic pain in this country. Twenty-three states and the District of Columbia have legalized marijuana to be used in medical treatments, called medical marijuana. This is quite a loose correlation involving the practice of medicine since most physicians are not familiar with how cannabinoids work or ideal strains and doses. The physician signs off by writing a letter of recommendation that states medical marijuana is good for the patient. The patient can then get a marijuana card and go to a dispensary. In this sense, marijuana is being treated as if it were an herbal with a blessing. This is good because that is its true nature. Those who dispense marijuana are not required to have any formal education related to specific diseases and marijuana. Preferably, this recommendation should specify which cannabinoids and doses are best. If your physician doesn't know about the specifics of marijuana's role in pain relief and the neighborhood marijuana dispensary has no real educational requirements, you must be your own advocate. A full discussion of the requirements and regulations of dispensaries will take place in Chapter 14. Let's review where the cannabinoids might relieve pain—and which are most apt to supplement our pain relief.

The first thing we need to consider is the form of these cannabinoids. Our options are the whole cannabis plant (marijuana or portions of this that include specific cannabinoids such as THC and CBD) or a combination of THC and CBD. Secondly, we must discuss the best method to get these chemicals into our body and the percentages thereof.

Example:

Component	Smoked (rolled joint)	Vapor-ized	Oral format	Pill	Food Mixture	%THC	%CBD
Marijuana	X					4%	4%
THC							0%
CBD mg						0%	___mg
THC/CBD mg's						___mg	___mg

In the example, we start with a joint with 4 % THC and 4% CBD. This is an average dose of THC and a high dose of CBD called Charlotte's Web. You may also start with only 1-2% THC if you are very sensitive to medications or new to marijuana.

What does 4% THC mean? Each gram has a dry weight of 1000mg. A 4% strain has 40mg of THC (.04 x 1000) in a gram. The Colorado mandate for edibles is limited to 10mg of THC per serving. A gram equals three joints on average. If this is at 10% THC, each joint contains 33mg of THC. There are twenty-eight grams in an ounce.

When you smoke marijuana, 50% of the THC content is in the smoke and the remaining 50% is exhaled, giving a yield of 25%. Some of the THC content is metabolized in the lungs. Blood levels are almost at a maximum after thirty to sixty seconds. Brain levels are not equivalent to blood levels because of the blood-brain barrier. Peak blood levels of THC are quickly metabolized and redistributed. Oral routes are absorbed one to three hours later.

Available THC is at 13-19%. Even though the blood level of THC delivered by smoke may peak at levels that are ten-times higher than that delivered orally, the brain level may only be a few times higher, which only lasts for a short time. Oro-mucosal spray may have a better absorption profile than orally-administered marijuana. Stacking of effects from THC can occur if many oral marijuana supplements are eaten over several hours. This can lead to excessive psychotropic feedback. Waiting until the full effect of the first dose (brownie) is recommended. Do not use marijuana products to ease your hunger. With this preliminary information, let's look at some studies.

Two different pain studies showed significant pain relief with THC. This, of course, worked on the CB 1 and CB 2 receptors. One study by Ware compared cannabis at 2.5%, 6%, and 9.4% THC against placebos. Statistically, 9.4% THC showed less pain than the placebo. There was no mention of the percent of CBD. A second study by Wilsey compared samples at 3.5% and 7% THC against placebos. Samples at 3.5% and 7% showed a statistical difference over placebo in the alleviating of pain intensity and unpleasantness. Wilsey also used a vapor format with samples at 1.29% and 3.5% THC against placebos. Both showed a statistical decrease in visual-analog scores that measure pain intensity over the placebo. It must be noted here that statistical significance may not translate into an equal amount of clinical significance in these cases. What constitutes a positive effect of a study is established prior to its initiation. Clinical significance can be a higher bar to reach.

Berman in 2004 used the cannabinoid extracts THC/CBD and THC, looking for pain relief and improved quality of sleep. Both showed statistically-significant reductions in intensity of pain and advancements in quality of sleep, but they did not reach clinical significance. As you recall, CBD does not work to any extent on CB 1 or CB 2 receptors. It has other pathways to anti-inflammation, but it also ameliorates the negative effects of THC. So. CBD's additional pain relief is a significant advantage.

In 2005 Rog found statistically-significant improvements in pain intensity and sleep disturbances using a THC/CBD extract. Nurmikko, in 2007, looked at neuropathic pain using Sativex (THC/CBD). He found reports of pain relief, with many patients getting over 30% relief. Initial pain relief was maintained without increasing doses at fifty-two weeks. Invasive procedures look for a reduction in symptoms of more than 50%, but drug trials usually look for 30%.

On the negative side, a trial on diabetic neuropathy in 2010 by Selvarajah used THC/CBD, and it found no difference between the drug and the placebo. A 2013 study by Langford, looking at the reduction of central neuropathic pain in MS with THC/CBD, was confusing. In the end, after much review, the study confirmed some relief with THC/CBD. The study looked at a central mediated neuropathic pain, which is more complicated than the peripheral form; also, there was a lingering question about dosing.

The side-effects in most of these studies were ones that are expected of any form of medication, including THC. The higher the THC percentage, the more side effects; this included sedation, confusion, disorientation, fatigue, headaches, impaired learning, and memory.

As we look over the information from these pain studies, I think we can say, with some certainty, there is evidence of relief through use of cannabinoids. However, we can't specify with certainty the ideal method of delivery or the efficacy of extracts versus whole cannabis products. The best way to handle this at this time is to think of marijuana as just another drug, whether or not it is prescribed. First, start with the lowest dose possible. In many of the studies, lower doses performed as well as higher doses. If you choose to smoke cannabis, then start with less than 2% THC and 4% CBD. If this is effective, stop there. The secondary (negative) side-effects seem to be rather prevalent at over 10%, so use less than 10% THC. If you decide to go with extracts, the extract Sativex, which was used in many of the studies, is not yet available in the US. It is a mixture of 2.7 mg THC and 2.5 mg CBD per spray bottle. The medications have an alcohol base. It may be available in the US in 2015 or early 2016. The price of this drug may be prohibitive for most. Other oils and extracts can be found at the neighborhood marijuana dispensary. These extracts eliminate the smoking-aspect, which is offensive to some. Rather than taking the THC and CBD, they may need to be taken separately. If marijuana products are not legal from a medical point of view in your state, CBD can be purchased online. The legality of CBD can be questioned, but it has an exemption in most states because it can come from hemp, which has no THC.

FLOW

What am I going to try (cannabis, THC, CBD, THC/CBD)? How it will be prepared (joint-smoked or vaporized, extract, pill format, edible)? What will the percentage or dosage be? Start low. How am I monitoring my side-effects and positive responses? Remember—cannabis is mostly an additive therapy. It is rarely meant to stand alone. Always be aware of your employer's position on the use of cannabis and drug tests. A medical marijuana card does not protect you from employer's rules and regulations. The federal government is in a bit of a holding pattern at this time concerning marijuana and its legality. Some states are moving forward with marijuana legalization even though it is a Schedule I drug under federal law. It's all very confusing and worrisome.

Chapter Twelve: Summary

- Marijuana has been used for pain relief for over 4,500 years.
- There are over 30 million people in the U.S. with chronic pain.
- A physician gives you a letter of recommendation for you to get a medical marijuana card; you then go to a dispensary, show your marijuana card, and obtain some marijuana. No one at the dispensary is required to be knowledgeable about marijuana and pain relief.
- You need to be knowledgeable about marijuana and pain relief.
- Be aware of how you want the marijuana delivered: joint, edibles, etc.
- Multiple studies show significant pain relief from cannabinoids.
- The side-effects from the cannabinoids rarely stopped any study participants from finishing the study.

Chapter Thirteen
Marijuana and PTSD

With the US's continuous involvement in active wars for the past dozen years, many of our soldiers (20-30%) return with PTSD (post-traumatic stress disorder). This has brought a major health issue to the forefront and spread awareness about how damaging it is. Of course, PTSD of some kind has been around since the beginning of mankind as we know it. PTSD is not only related to war, but all other forms of trauma. It is brought on by either witnessing or participating in an event that is terrifying and potentially life-threatening. These events can cause severe anxiety, continual flashbacks, nightmares, and uncontrollable thoughts. The severity of the symptoms is variable, which can last for years after the precipitating event. The symptoms can be expressed emotionally and/or physically. The emotional symptoms include depression, guilt, worry, and a feeling of emptiness. The physical symptoms can manifest neurologically or in the cardiac and respiratory systems.

There are several current drug treatments for PTSD. Two antidepressants in particular have been approved for use against PTSD: Zoloft and Paxil. Occasionally a benzodiazepine will be prescribed to help with sleep or anxiety. These medications have many side-effects. There is a search for better and more complementary therapies to enable lower doses. Since PTSD patients appear to have increased sympathetic output and changes in memory-processing (reliving events), there have been attempts to block sympathetic output. Use of cannabis products has been proposed as a solution. The cannabinoids have many qualities that might give necessary relief from the numbing effects of PTSD.

The use of cannabis products in PTSD should be under the supervision of a physician. Self-treatment is not recommended. The use of cannabis in treatment and its relationship to possible conflict with administrative regulations on the job must be kept in mind. Obtaining PTSD treatment involving cannabis under the supervision of a VA physician may be difficult, and outside treatment may be necessary.

Increasing coping mechanisms and quality of sleep are two of the most-common reasons people with PTSD use some form of cannabis. The potential for drug abuse is very high in some-one with ongoing, severe PTSD. Self-medicating and self-dosing are continuous concerns.

At a 2012 conference on cannabis therapeutics sponsored by Patients Out of Time, Mashiah made a presentation about PTSD and Israeli soldiers. They were given a fixed amount of cannabis to use per month and told to use it at their own pace. Cannabis use did not stop the PTSD, but it did lessen the symptoms. J Psychoactive Drugs published a paper in 2014 by Greer that looked at eighty patients who had PTSD with and without cannabis. The paper looked at the symptoms of re-experiencing, avoidance-numbing, and hyperarousal. This study, which was probably biased, did not have a placebo, but it showed a reduction of the symptoms measured in their group.

The measurements for determining PTSD are done by a test called the CAPS-5. This is a clinician-administered PTSD scale for DSM-5. It is called the gold standard in PTSD assessment. Both of the studies about PTSD used this method. CAPs-5 is a questionnaire with thirty questions that comes up with a severity score. There are three versions: past week, past month, worst month.

The verdict is still out on whether or not cannabis is another answer to PTSD symptoms. It is clear that it deserves to be studied. Individual patients with severe PTSD may be candidates for closely-monitored use. Self-medicating for PTSD without the supervision of a knowledgeable physician is not recommended. The studies are few but promising. PTSD is a huge problem, so pursuing this line of research is essential. For the federal government, this is a serious dilemma. Schedule I status says marijuana is without medical value and illegal, but studies show it is therapeutic for soldiers with PTSD.

Chapter Thirteen: Summary

- Cannabinoids have many properties that can lead to routine therapy for PTSD.
- Those who suffer from PTSD turn to cannabis to increase coping mechanisms and improve sleep quality.
- Several studies show cannabis reduces symptoms. The use of cannabis to reduce the symptoms of PTSD seems promising.
- Using marijuana in PTSD without supervision is not recommended.

Chapter Fourteen
Marijuana and the Law: At Home and At Work

Nothing about marijuana is more confusing than its legal aspects. There are few things we are absolutely sure of, including that marijuana is still a Schedule I drug as far as the federal government is concerned. This essentially says that marijuana is in a class with the most dangerous drugs—and has no medical value. Contrary to this ruling by the FDA and DEA, twenty-three states and the District of Columbia made marijuana available for medical uses. The federal government has relaxed its enforcement of some aspects of its laws in these states.

Two sets of divergent laws rarely coexist this way. There is a substantial amount of current evidence for medical uses of marijuana. Some touted uses are backed by weak, but many are backed by solid evidence. In most instances, marijuana is far-less dangerous than alcohol or tobacco.

In the late 1920's, due to a confluence of circumstances, marijuana became a targeted drug. This was after over 4,500 years of its being used for recreation or medical treatments. In 1937, a federal tax was placed on the use of marijuana, and failure to pay this tax was punished with a fine or jail-time. The states followed suit by passing their own anti-narcotic laws. This was not because the drug was dangerous; it was a monetary, racial, and political issue. It was made a Schedule I drug in 1970.

In 2012, Colorado and Washington passed a measure to permit recreational/medical use of marijuana. In 2014, Alaska, Oregon, and the District of Columbia followed suit. It's as if the federal statute does not even exist in these states. The following states have medical marijuana measures in place: Alaska, Arizona, California, Colorado, Connecticut, Washington D.C., Delaware, Hawaii, Illinois, Maine, Maryland, Massachusetts, Michigan, Minnesota, Montana, Nevada, New Hampshire, New Jersey, New Mexico, New York, Oregon, Rhode Island, Vermont, and Washington. In November 2015, Ohio voted against a measure that would permit medical and recreational marijuana. It seems as if the measure failed because the focus was more about money than marijuana. Perhaps medical and recreational uses should be separated, not combined on a ballot measure.

Slightly less than half of drug arrests (about 800,000) are still for marijuana possession, not intent to sell. The rate of use of marijuana among African Americans is equal to the rate among whites, but African Americans are three-times more likely to be arrested and convicted. For African Americans, this discrepancy has not been overlooked. The history of marijuana is closely tied to racism. In particular, this related to African Americans and Hispanics. This racism, the recent seventy-year history of marijuana, the drug wars, and a lack of education about marijuana all helped to keep its Schedule I status. It is time to replace the Schedule I status with my proposed status: herb with an asterisk.

Even though recreational use is legal in some states, all states have limits for possession. These limits vary by state. Several states have only legalized smoke-free cannabis, including

New York and Minnesota. For the most part, the legal limits of possession of cannabis are modest, except Oregon, where the legal limit is twenty-four usable ounces. This is almost five-times the average state legal limit.

The Dutch have a functional policy on drugs. It focuses on individual health, less public nuisance, and drug-related crime. This can fit well into our marijuana policy. There is little evidence that low doses of cannabis on an occasional basis causes any major health issues for adults. If you already have heath issues, think hard about the use of marijuana. Common sense should prevail. There are anecdotal reports that legalizing marijuana reduces some violent crimes. This reduction may or may not be tied to legalization. More information is necessary.

In 2012, an embarrassing presentation to Congress was delivered by an administrator from the DEA. Michele Leonhart, a DEA administrator, made statements about marijuana that were not true. She had essentially tossed marijuana in with crack and methamphetamines. It was obvious that she had not researched the thousands of research articles and papers on marijuana. The risk of mortality from marijuana use is lower than for both tobacco and alcohol use. The risk of fatal overdose is almost unheard of. The public health burden of marijuana is loosely-calculated at less than 10% of either tobacco or alcohol. A noted and well-respected neurosurgeon and journalist for CNN, Dr. Sanjay Gupta, has apologized on air for his prior stance on medical marijuana. He clarified that he had not studied the topic fully, and he saw the distinct possibilities of using marijuana in medicine. This is what I believe has happened—and is still happening—to marijuana. If you really study marijuana, the possibilities become clear and the true nature of the drug comes to light.

Several more states will have marijuana on the ballots in 2016. It would be good to see more states give people the freedom to use marijuana, at least for medical use. The laws should include moderate legal limits for possession, and possibly, a maximum THC percentage of 10%. Percentages above 10% only exist for the sake of getting high, which can be done at levels at or below 10%, thus promoting psychological safety. A November 2015 study in Psychological Medicine called "Effect of high-potency cannabis on corpus callosum microstructure" showed frequent use of high-potency cannabis is associated with disturbed callosal microstructure. The corpus callosum has a role in interhemispheric connectivity, and it is part of the white matter of the brain.

Drug testing at the workplace continues to be an issue. There is a lot of misunderstanding, and many raise the question of personal rights. The use of drug testing stems from the employer's interest in workplace safety. There are no federal laws against drug testing. The other common reasons for employers to implement policies are: deter employees from abusing drugs, have knowledge of drug use prior to hiring, early identification of possible drug abuse, to comply with state or federal regulations, and discounts from Workers Compensation premiums.

The Federal government leaves most of these laws up to the states except for DOT, military, and the nuclear industry. SAMSHA (Substance Abuse and Mental Health Services Administration) has set up drug testing criteria for the federal government. Many private companies follow these rules to avoid legal entanglements. State and local governments also regulate a significant number of these laws. Laws regarding drug testing provide for specific notification, specific procedures for testing, and handling test samples. There are about 650 state laws regarding drug testing and 10,000 related court decisions. In a unionized workplace, parts of the drug testing policy are negotiated in contracts. The Supreme Court is usually divided when these issues are brought before them, indicating this is a complex maze, not a simple process. The segments are broken down below.

Applicant

Applicant is aware drug screening will be done for employment, job offer contingent on passing drug test, all applicants are tested in a similar fashion, and tests are performed at a state-certified lab.

Current Employee

State laws are quite varied. Some states do not allow random-testing in private companies (the federal government does random-testing). If a state allows random-testing, it should be clearly random and sent to a state-certified lab. Incident-related drug testing, including testing in response to an accident, is allowed in all states.

Challenging results

You can refuse to take a drug test. You can be fired for not taking the test, and you can potentially lose unemployment benefits because of this refusal. The employer only has to show good cause (reasonable suspicion) to ask for testing. Examples of reasonable suspicion include: observed drug use at work, erratic behavior, worsening job performance, reported drug use with corroboration, causing or contributing an accident, and things specific to a particular job.

Marijuana is detected more frequently than any other drug in drug tests. The percentage of positive tests is 2.1% for nonsensitive jobs and 0.67% for safety-sensitive jobs (such as DOT). About 60% of employers give drug tests and 40% do not as part of pre-employment criteria. 90% of these employers continue periodic testing. Most (over 85%) of drug tests are simple urine tests because it is easy to do at the workplace. Post-employment drug tests are random, prompted by reasonable suspicion, or done in response to an accident testing.

Around 6-8% of workers used marijuana last month. A higher percentage of younger workers, and a lower percentage of workers with a higher education, use marijuana. 2.5% of workers are dependent on drugs.

Samhsa Guidelines To Insure Accuracy And Validity Of Samples:

1. Chain of Custody—a chain of custody is used to document the handling and storage of a sample from the time of collection to the time of disposal.
2. Initial Screen—this is the first analysis done on a sample. If a test is positive, then a second confirmation test is run.
3. Confirmation test—a second confirmation test is run on a gas chromatograph or mass spectrometer. This is highly accurate.
4. Split sample—the initial urine sample is split in two. One sample is used for the initial test and the second sample is used for the confirmation test.

Different Tests Used For Analysis:

- Urine—simply to show the presence or absence of a drug or metabolites. It does not show you are currently under the influence of a drug, but it does show that you used a drug in the last few days.

- Breathe—just for alcohol. 0.08 is the normal limit for normal circumstances (0.02 for DOT).
- Blood—shows drugs that are currently physiologically-active in the body. Blood levels of cannabinoids do not correlate well with impairment, but they can be interpreted as evidence of impairment.
- Hair—this provides a longer testing window than any of the other methods. Theoretically, it can detect usage up to 90 days before. Marijuana use can be detected this way. Not done as an impairment test, just evidence of prior use.
- Sweat—this drug detection is usually in the form of a patch. It is worn by parolees or employees on probation to detect drug use. THC in marijuana can be detected by a patch.

The usual five drugs covered in these tests are: amphetamines, THC, cocaine, opiates and phencyclidine. Remember, acute marijuana use is gone in about three days, and it is rarely detected; chronic use may be detected up to several weeks later.

Dispensaries

Dispensaries are a large part of getting the product to the consumer. Let's take a look at some regulations. California is a good state to start with because they have been in the medical-marijuana dispensing business as long as any other. Just to be clear, in the eyes of the federal government, marijuana dispensaries are illegal. At present, they are not prosecuting. When administrations—or parties in power—change, there is always concern about policy changes. This is why we need to drop the Schedule I status of marijuana and change its status back to an herb. Who qualifies for medical marijuana in California? Anyone with cancer, anorexia, migraines, AIDS, chronic pain, spasticity, glaucoma, or any illness that marijuana might relieve.

In 2004, California further clarified its law. An ID card was established that allowed the holder to cultivate, possess, and transport up to eight ounces of dried, processed marijuana and six mature or twelve immature plants. Patients may be exempt if their physician states they need more. This bill also legalized collective and cooperative cultivation of marijuana. Distribution for profit was not part of this bill.

First, a seller's permit must be obtained from the state. Marijuana sold is subject to sales tax. The individual counties and cities where the dispensary is to be located might have further permits. There needs to be a process at the dispensary where each patient (or primary caregiver) completes an application. The physician name and patient's contact information need to be on the front of the application. The information on the application also needs to be verified. The applicant needs to sign an agreement, thereby agreeing to not distribute marijuana or use marijuana for anything except medical purposes.

Medical marijuana cooperatives can only purchase marijuana from members of their co-op. The marijuana must be grown by a qualified patient/caregiver. The cooperative must remain a non-profit. Neighborhood complaints are the biggest reason for any police harassment. If you are a good neighbor, there will be no police.

Again, this is a state that only has medical marijuana. Other states, such as Oregon, can sell recreational marijuana without the name of the purchaser. There is a daily legal limit of the amount of marijuana that can be purchased. Without a name, this seems to be a difficult proposition. Any registered medical marijuana dispensary can sell recreational marijuana in Oregon.

I don't mean to infer that legalizing marijuana is a simple process. We got off-track seventy years ago, but this doesn't mean we shouldn't fix it. The thoughts that go into legalization are a compromise between potential harm and restrictions placed on individuals. If we look at the harm alcohol and tobacco caused and compare it with marijuana, then marijuana would win hands-down. There are many steps in legalization. Assuring they are all in place will waylay any unintended negative results. The laws about legal possession limits become fines and community service (racial bias must be removed), making clear the maximum amount of THC in edibles and considering the possible revision of workplace testing results. The FDA needs to remove the Schedule I status from marijuana to align with state laws. Marijuana research needs to be funded, forums for public education about marijuana need to be scheduled, and medical schools need to educate their physicians so they understand how marijuana can help their patients. In most of states that legalized marijuana, there were several steps left out that made the transition of adding marijuana to their culture, making the legalities more difficult.

Before any consideration of less-stringent workplace regulations about marijuana, a better understanding of several characteristic responses to THC are necessary. This would be true for medical marijuana in particular. Included in this are responses to THC percentages and related doses, frequency, and methods of use. If the responses to these are known, then a quantitative measure of THC can be used for non-safety related workplace environments that test for marijuana. Is there a level of marijuana that can be permitted for non-safety jobs?

Chapter Fourteen: Summary

- Laws regulating marijuana are inconsistent. It is considered an illegal Schedule I drug by the federal government. Twenty-three states have legalized medical marijuana, and four of these have legalized recreational marijuana. This will come to a head soon. We need to get the FDA to change the Schedule I status.
- The Dutch have a more consistent drug policy; a policy we should look at in depth. It focuses on individual health and reducing public nuisance and drug-related crime.
- We desperately need to educate our politicians and law-enforcement about the pluses and minuses of marijuana. Clarifying that alcohol and tobacco are much worse for you is a start.
- Drug testing is legal, but a very well-defined and strict process needs to be in place. With the potential legalization of recreational marijuana, these workplace drug standards might need some revision. If you are going to use drugs and work, you should be familiar with the SAMHSA guidelines
- Dispensaries in California operate effectively. California can be a model for other states.

Chapter Fifteen
Does the Use of Marijuana Lead to Use of Other Drugs?

Is marijuana a gateway drug that leads to more dangerous and addictive drugs? There was an article from 2010 on Time Magazine's website by Szalavitz entitled "Marijuana as a Gateway Drug: The Myth that will not die". This is a good title to introduce this discussion. Opponents of marijuana commonly argue it is a gateway drug. However, saying something doesn't make it true. Let's start our discussion by looking at the scientific definition of a gateway substance.

The hypothesis is that the use of soft drugs/substances including alcohol, tobacco, or cannabis will subsequently lead to hard drugs (cocaine, heroin, and methamphetamines). The first problem with this is the lack of clarity. Are we trying to say that this drug, upon arriving in our body, somehow forces us to use hard drugs? Some studies say only 33% of marijuana users move on to hard drugs. What happened to the transformation in the other 67%? This transformation and relationship is backed by loose evidence. If this hypothesis is false, then another proposal is needed. How about the concept that the use of this drug gives us confidence that we can handle harder drugs because marijuana was easy? This aspect may need to involve peer groups and social interactions. This may be a necessity due to some difficulty in obtaining hard drugs. Peers might actually help buy the drugs, or they might be dealers themselves. So, is it the initial drug that led to the use of hard drugs, or the environment? The example with Hell's Angels is one of my favorites. Suppose Hell's Angels all rode bikes as kids, which led them to motorcycles and ultimately to the Hell's Angels. Did riding bikes as kids cause them to become Hell's Angels?

In the US, there is some data that cocaine users all started with marijuana. This is a mere inversion of the argument presented earlier. Should this not be true for all countries that have cocaine problems? In Japan the use of cocaine is not usually preceded by marijuana use. Is there something about the flow of substances in the US that can explain this? Alcohol and tobacco use almost always precede the use of marijuana. A gateway theory shouldn't start with the third substance in the list for defining a gateway. In Japan, amphetamines are used more than any other illicit drug. Marijuana use is low, and it has no connection with cocaine use.

Several studies, in their discussion-phase, believe that alcohol is the real culprit. This classifies alcohol as the original gateway. Preventing the use of hard substances should start by preventing alcohol use among young teens. Alcohol, tobacco, and marijuana are unsafe for teens. Each of them has a unique way of changing development. We discussed the very negative effects of marijuana in adolescents in Chapter 4.

The gateway theories avoid the truth—that we do not understand the causal relationship that may lead to hard drugs, between drugs, ourselves, and our environment. Some use drugs to escape reality. Some use them to deal with peer pressure. Tobacco and alcohol are built into our society. Tobacco is losing ground; over 50% of the population smoked in the 1960's, but now only 19% do. Alcohol is a centerpiece in American life. 60% of adults drink alcohol on a regular basis. If alcohol is the real gateway, can it be kept from our youth? Maybe it's all just a psychological problem relating to the mental state of the user/abuser—just don't blame marijuana. The answer may be closer to home.

Chapter Fifteen: Summary

- Marijuana is not a gateway drug. If you insist on finding one, look at either alcohol or tobacco.

Chapter Sixteen
Marijuana: Addiction and Withdrawl

First, let's clarify the terms addiction and withdrawal. Addiction is a condition that results when a person uses a substance and the act of using the substance becomes compulsive. This compulsion interferes with life's responsibilities. Addicts may not be aware of their behavior. Their behavior is usually a problem for the addict and those around them. The addiction can be either physical or psychological. Physical adaptation to a drug implies the body has developed a need for the drug. The psychological addiction is more difficult. It may not be based on the drug's effects on the body or the brain. Switching addictions—from one substance to another—is common in this case.

Withdrawal is a syndrome that includes cessation of drug use and the resultant over-activity of the physiological functions of the body. Symptoms include irritability, depression, anxiety, sleep problems, decreased or increased appetite, stomach pain, tremors, sweating, fever, and chills.

Addiction to marijuana can potentially happen to anyone. Higher probability of addiction coincides with early users. 10% of users become addicted on average. This 10% rate is almost the same for alcohol and opioids. Those who started in their teens face greater risk at 20%. In 2013, 60% of drug addiction involved marijuana. Just slightly less than 30% of admissions to drug programs for marijuana addiction were between twelve and seventeen years old. There is much concern over the increases in THC content and the connection to increased addiction.

Addiction to marijuana can manifest itself by the need to restart the drug. The typical story starts with someone deciding to stop smoking marijuana. The first couple of days don't seem to be too big of a deal. In the following days, many withdrawal symptoms appear. THC in the blood drops below therapeutic levels. The brain got used to the cannabinoids, especially THC, and overreacts to this absence. This overreaction can include bizarre dreams, moodiness, or depression. After several weeks, many decide to return to the use of marijuana to waylay the symptoms.

To lower the sting of being called an addict, "cannabis use disorder" now describes this addiction. It sounds better—but not calling a spade a spade doesn't change what it is. There are eleven criteria for this disorder:

- Using more or for a longer period than intended
- Persistent desire to cut back
- Lots of time spent using
- Craving, strong urges to use
- Use contributes to failures at work, school, and home
- Continued use despite recurrent interpersonal or social problems related to use
- Use leads to giving up or reducing important social, occupational, or recreational activities
- Recurrent use in hazardous situations
- Continued use despite recurrent physical or psychological problems related to use

- Tolerance
- Withdrawal

Two or three symptoms indicate mild addiction; four to five symptoms indicate moderate addiction; and six or more symptoms indicate severe addiction. The terminology is somewhat in a state of flux. There are two terms at play: addictive dependence and non-addictive abuse. In other words, you can abuse marijuana, but not necessarily be addicted to it. It seems addictive dependence is more related to personal addiction (physical and psychological), and non-addictive abuse has more to do with the consequences of overuse including trouble with the law, losing friends, and aggression. Marijuana addicts also have their own twelve-step program called Marijuana Anonymous.

Let's look closer at withdrawal. The usual symptoms of marijuana withdrawal are increasing anxiety, irritability, restlessness, and sleep difficulties (falling asleep or intense dreams). These symptoms are both physical and psychological. They will occur in about 80% of chronic, heavy users who try to stop. The usual opioid withdrawal symptoms of chills, stomach cramps, shakiness, and sweating are seldom present.

Typical treatment avenues for marijuana addiction/dependence have a psychosocial bend. There has been recent interest in using cannabinoid receptor agonists to treat marijuana withdrawal. This type of approach is not novel; it is used in tobacco (nicotine patches) and opioids (methadone for heroin). The rationale for substituting an agonist is simple. It is usually a safer drug, and the route of administration is safer. By using this agonist-replacement drug, people can use lower levels of the offending drug—if not stop completely. Sativex, which is a combination of THC and CBD, was studied by Allsop (April

2015, American Society for Clinical Pharmacology and Therapeutics) for assistance with withdrawal from marijuana. Sativex is a metered-spray form for oromucosal use. Sativex was discussed in Chapter 10 for use in MS. They found it useful in suppressing withdrawal symptoms among in-patients. Further studies to clarify dosing and discover how long the agonist should be used are ongoing.

Drugs like gabapentin have also helped with the symptoms of withdrawal. The key thing to remember is that dealing with the initial physical withdrawal is the simplest part. The psychological aspect has to be met with many lifestyle changes. Marijuana became your best friend.

It is clear that addiction to marijuana can rival any other drug for its persistence against sustained withdrawal. The relapse rate can be as high as 80%. This makes it clear that current treatment has a long way to go before it can be classified as a success. Many treatment centers set a goal that includes moderate use of marijuana, a step down from heavy use.

Chapter Sixteen: Summary

- You can become addicted to marijuana.
- Withdrawal from marijuana is a reality and the withdrawal itself can cause many to relapse.
- Current treatment for addiction and subsequent withdrawal does not have a high success rate.
- New agonist treatments for marijuana withdrawal have shown some success.
- Awareness that heavy sustained use of marijuana can be addictive is critical to continued use.
- The majority of marijuana users do not experience problems.
- Only about 10% of people with addiction problems seek help.

Chapter Seventeen
Do You Need Marijuana or
Can You Pick Your Cannabinoids?

Is it better to have all the cannabinoids working together, as in marijuana, or picking one or two to meet your needs? This question deals more with the medical marijuana debate than the recreational debate. Of the over 1,600 articles I read for this book, 150 of them mentioned the real possibility of cannabinoids in marijuana work together. By working together, the cannabinoids act in a synergistic manner, which is somewhat regulatory. The regulatory aspect is shown in how CBD ameliorates many of the negative effects of THC. Several studies, in their discussion phase, alluded to the possibility that CBD's presence strengthened the positive effects of THC.

In the world of marijuana, this sum of the whole is called the entourage effect. Most long-time users swear that this entourage effect is true. In fact, they call the separation of the cannabinoids a creation of an inferior medicine. Let's break this question down to see if there are any clear answers.

Is marijuana as a whole better than its parts? This is probably true. The problem with this answer is it does not take into consideration why you are taking marijuana. If you are taking it for spasticity, then it may be true. If you are taking marijuana for arthritis, then it may not be true. With arthritis, you need an overwhelming amount of CBD while THC doesn't matter.

Why not always use marijuana as a whole? Anytime you use less drugs/chemicals, and remain close to the same effect, it is always a better plan. Do not forget those over 400 chemicals and 60-80 cannabinoids in marijuana. Specific cannabinoids should be considered. In children who need marijuana products smoking is rarely an option. The exposure of children to THC should be avoided due to its effect on a developing brain. THC and CBD work well together, and as a team they can loosely mimic the whole plant.

If it can't be smoked, can alternative methods of delivery be as effective? Maybe. There is no better way to deliver the cannabinoids of marijuana than inhalation. This can be smoking a joint or vaporizing. The percentage of delivery does depend on knowing how to breath, hold your breath, and then exhale less-than-normal volumes. It all depends on getting the chemicals into your blood, which then can get them to receptors throughout your body, including your brain. Oral absorption is variable, and it delivers a low percentage of the original dose. Oromucosal helps increase absorption. Other methods can deliver levels comparable to inhalation. This can approximate the effectiveness of smoking marijuana.

Chapter Seventeen: Summary

- The cannabinoids of marijuana appear to be synergistic.
- Smoking marijuana is the best delivery system, but other methods can come close.
- Some chemicals of marijuana can be avoided by not using the whole plant, but with a drop in the effectiveness.
- THC and CBD together are a viable alternative to the whole plant if necessary.

Chapter Eighteen
There's Marijuana and There's Political Marijuana

Restrictions were placed on marijuana well before most potential side-effects were known. Over 4,500 years of legal use of marijuana ground to a halt when it was made a Schedule I drug in 1970 by congress/FDA. This was a political and racist decision. The racist beginnings of these laws from the 1930's continued to be perpetuated. Harry Anslinger, the first commissioner of the Federal Bureau of Narcotics, did more damage to marijuana (and African American males) with his racist views than any science or ad campaign could. He was in office from 1930-1962, a significant amount of time for significant damage. There were little, if any, facts involved. Marijuana became the most important illicit drug in the US. The return of marijuana to the marketplace, achieved with votes in twenty-three states, was equally about money and medicine. States collect massive amounts of taxes on marijuana sales.

We have discussed the negative side-effects of marijuana, including addiction and cognitive impairment. We also discussed some of the wonderful ways marijuana can help with many medical conditions. These are actually superfluous to the current situation. The FDA, instead of changing the status of marijuana to a Schedule II drug or an alternative medicine pre-scribed by a medical provider, did nothing. Now, we have states legalizing its use for medical and recreational purposes. There is no mandatory limit of THC. There is no mandatory educa-tion for medical personnel. There is no mandatory funding set aside from the huge profits for research. Legal limits can exceed a six-month's supply in some states. There are many laws ad-dressing the quality of the plants; what a mess.

Marijuana has always had followers—legal or not. The recreational use of marijuana was never really curtailed by all the laws. What was curtailed in a big way was medical use and research. The FDA could have given many universities the abil-ity to study marijuana further, and its potential could be clari-fied. The 1990's, when the endocannabinoid system was elucidated, was the perfect time to fund research. The cannabi-noids, which so many fight against, occur naturally in the human body.

Many of the purposes of government protect us from our-selves. In the case of marijuana, the federal government created a problem when they made marijuana a Schedule I drug; it then proceeded to put millions of people in prison, which cost bil-lions of dollars, because of that decision. The drug war cam-paign also stripped over 100,000 people from their right to vote because of unbelievably-small possession charges. These were mostly African American males. The lobbyists for the marijuana groups were almost non-existent at the federal level. It was much easier to lobby at a state level. This is evidenced by the huge success of witnessing twenty-three states pass some sort of marijuana legislation. These state laws permitting medical marijuana had almost zero restrictions on THC percentages—or what medical marijuana even is.

The focus on community education about marijuana is lacking, even in most of the states where it is legal. Everyone should know about the negative effects of marijuana during pregnancy. Everyone should know about the potentially-negative effects of marijuana on our adolescents. Dangerously-high levels of THC need consideration. Medical schools in states where marijuana is legal have done little to educate their student physicians on dosing, side-effects, and their responsibility. The American Medical Association (AMA), which is a very powerful lobby, should demand that the FDA allow universities to study marijuana without repercussions.

Hopefully, we will elect officials who will demand changes in legislation on marijuana use. Start with the US. Congress; elect officials who have actually read about marijuana. Next, move on to the FDA; change the status of marijuana to a designation that fits its possible benefits to us. In this order, law enforcement would be next. Violations should be changed to community service and possession should never lead to jail-time.

There are many scientific books out there about marijuana; read any of them. The facts speak for themselves. The government overstepped its boundaries. This led to many other bad decisions. Let's gather more information with quality research from universities. Reclassification of marijuana as an herb, without the risk of jail-time, is not out of the question.

Chapter Eighteen: Summary

- The federal government needs to lead the way in the reclassification of marijuana.
- Much of the negative chatter about marijuana is unfounded. There are side-effects we are aware of. There needs to be public education about marijuana.
- The response to marijuana by the federal government did not match the behavior or the toxicity of the drug. Imprisonment for possession is absurd; its a racist policy that disproportionately incarcerates African Americans.
- The AMA should take the lead in educational efforts with support from individuals and communities.
- Our Congressmen should read a book on marijuana. I made this one short enough to be read on a flight from Washington D. C. to Los Angeles.

Chapter Nineteen
What Does It All Add Up To?

Have you ever wondered why the cannabis plant produces almost eighty different cannabinoids? Humans have only found use for maybe four or five of them. There are no cannabinoid receptors like ours in the cannabis plant. There are several suppositions about what some of the cannabinoids do for the cannabis plant. One of these is to protect it from UV light. I find this interesting because of the over 1,500 articles reviewed for this book, none of them looked at marijuana being used as a sunscreen. I wonder, if over 4,000 years ago when marijuana was first being used, was the brain as full of cannabinoid receptors as it is now?

When you think about marijuana, think about our own endocannabinoid system. Our brain is full of cannabinoid receptors (CB 1) and the rest of our body has CB1s and CB 2s. We have our own cannabinoids. Our cannabinoids work at the same receptors as marijuana's cannabinoids—the same, exact receptors. Our endocannabinoid system works to regulate many of our daily functions. Don't stop thinking about the relationship between marijuana cannabinoids, our cannabinoids, and our receptors. It's more natural than you think.

As you read the chapter on medical marijuana, how could you consider it a Schedule I drug? Remember, a Schedule I drug is one that has no medical benefit. If we remove the politicians who are racist and/or who do very little reading from the room, marijuana goes back to being an herb. It has been an herb for over 4,500 years and needs to return to its rightful place.

Marijuana is an herb, but we know more about this herb. It is not good for a fetus or the developing brain of a child or adolescent. We must take care to ensure that this is common knowledge.

Research has been hampered by the laws hanging over marijuana. Those against marijuana say there is not enough evidence for medical use. In the same breath, they deny funding for research and access to marijuana, which can clarify the issues. Do we really need higher and higher percentages of THC in our medical marijuana? It can be concentrated if there is a special medical need. No medical need appeared to require over 10%. Why do we have levels at 20%? Higher percentages are more physically and mentally dangerous. The risk-benefit ratio disappears with higher percentages of THC. Dispensing marijuana for medical use with THC over 10% is not medical marijuana. With the recent article from October 2015 in Psychological Medicine looking at the negative effects on the corpus callosum of our brain from high THC levels, there may be significant liability for anyone dispensing it as medical marijuana. Risk of addiction correlates with higher percentages of THC.

The number of people in prison for possession is part of the failed anti-drug war. Possession sentences should be taken off the books and expunged.

Marijuana can be addictive, and it does have a form of withdrawal. With recognition, skills, and the correct treatment, it can be treated over time.

Your skill set when you are using marijuana is not normal. Reaction times and cognitive processes are impaired. Driving under the influence of marijuana is hardly different from driving under the influence of alcohol. Fatal auto accidents related to marijuana are on the rise.

Care needs to be exercised if you use marijuana and have medical conditions including heart disease, cerebral-vascular disease, or hypertension. You should factor your physician's input when deciding whether or not it is safe for you to use.

It may be true that having marijuana available will significantly reduce opioid deaths. The 2014 JAMA article by Bachhuber showed a 24% reduction in opioid deaths in states were marijuana was legalized. With the use of marijuana for chronic pain, the use of opioids decreases.

Ohio just defeated (November 2015) a measure to legalize medical and recreational marijuana. They did two things wrong. First, they took on medical and recreational marijuana at the same time. Even California didn't do that. Secondly, it seemed to be more about money than marijuana. Ten big interests would have controlled it all. Make it about the marijuana.

Synthetic marijuana, like spice, is not an option. It is way too dangerous and it has no quality control whatsoever.

Hillary Clinton, while running for president in 2016, stated her position on marijuana was a-wait-and-see approach. She would wait and see what happens in the four states with recreational marijuana. We need to be aware that marijuana can be approved, but having some common sense restrictions in place is imperative. The headlines from a federally-funded impact study on Colorado legalization was not positive for marijuana. The headlines said the study showed an increase in marijuana-related traffic deaths, school suspensions, lab explosions, and hospital visits. Marijuana has a distinct place in our society, but abuse is not the answer.

Let's continue to move forward with state legalized marijuana, at least for medical uses. While we're working at the state level, inundate the FDA and your politicians in Washington DC to change the status of marijuana's classification as a Schedule I drug. A few restrictions may need to be in place, such as a limits of THC for medical use. Marijuana has a place in medicine. It is not a cure all. It needs to be used as a complimentary medicine. Let's also demand that the people selling marijuana in dispensaries have a minimum amount of education related to their products effects on people. This would stop them from selling products like skunk (20% THC and no CBD) for medical use.

Bibliography

Chapter One

Drug Science.org Discovery of the Cannabinoid System 2006

Colbert M Indica, Sativa, and Ruderalis- Did we get it all wrong? Science Jan 2015

Chapter Two

Cannabis Encyclopedia: Cannabis Research A-Z

Sulak D Introduction to the Endocannabinoid System. 2010

Chapter Three

Drug Testing Book: Cannabinoid pharmacokinetics

Toennes SW Comparison of Cannabinoid Pharmacokinetic Properties on Occasional and Heavy Users Smoking a Marijuana or Placebo Joint. Journal of Analytical Toxicology Sept 2008

Su MK Metabolism of classical cannabinoids and the synthetic cannabinoid JWH-018. Clinical Pharmacology and Therapeutics Apr 2015

Sharma P Chemistry, Metabolism, and Toxicology of Cannabis: Clinical Implications. Iran J Psychiatry Fall 2012

Vermuri VK Medicinal chemistry of cannabinoids. Clinical Pharmacology and Therapeutics Apr 2015

Gertsch J Phytocannabinoids beyond the Cannabis plant- do they exist? J Pharmacol June 2010

Forensic Science and Medicine: Marijuana and the Cannabinoids Chapter 2 e Editor Elsohly MA

Chapter Four

Kosty DB Parental transmission of risk for cannabis use disorder to offspring. Addiction Apr 2015

Warner TD It's not your Mother's Marijuana. Clinics in perinatology Dec 20 J 14

Conner SN Maternal marijuana use and neonatal morbidity. Am J Obstet Gynecol2015; 213

Hurd YL Marijuana impairs growth in mid-gestation fetuses. Neurotoxicology and Teratology Dec 2004

Crocker CE Cannabis and the maturing brain: Role in psychosis development. Clin Pharmacology and Therapeutics June 2015

Porath-Waller AJ Young brains on cannabis: It's time to clear the smoke. Clin Pharmacol June 2015

Day NL The effects of prenatal marijuana exposure on delinquent behaviors are mediated by measures of neurocognitive functioning. Neurotoxicology and Teratology Jan 2011

Chapter Five

None

Chapter Six

Kemp A Top 10 facts you should know. Synthetic cannabinoids: not so nice spice. Miss State Med Assoc. May 2015

Bolognini D Medical cannabis vs synthetic cannabinoids: What does the future hold? Clin, Pharmacology and Therapeutics May 2015

Mills B Synthetic Cannabinoids. American Journal for the Medical Sciences July 2015

Gunderson EW Synthetic Cannabinoids: A New Frontier of Designer Drugs. Ann Intern Med 2013; 159

National Institute on Drug Abuse Drugfacts: K2/Spice (Synthetic Marijuana. Dec 2012

Chapter Seven

Munivappa R Metabolic Effects of Chronic Cannabis Smoking. Diabetes Care Aug 2013

Braver O Cannabinoid Hyperemesis Syndrome. IMAJ May 2015

Pletcher MJ Association between Marijuana Exposure and Pulmonary Function Over 20 Years. JAMA Jan 2012

Gash AD Effects of Smoking Marijuana on Left Ventricular Performance and Plasma Norepinephrine. Ann Intern Med1978; 89

Editorial Does Marijuana affect Viral Loads in people with HIV? Ann Intern Med Aug 2003

Filbey FM Long term effects of marijuana on the brain. Pro. Natl. Aced. Sci. USA Nov 2014

Thanvi BR Cannabis and Stroke: is there a link? Postgrad Med J 2009;85

Villares J Chronic use of marijuana decreases cannabinoid receptor binding and mRNA expression in the human brain. Neuroscience Mar 2003

Chapter Eight

Whiting PF Cannabinoids for medical Use: A Systematic Review and meta-analysis. JAMA 2015:31

Malik Z The role of Cannabinoids in Regulation of Nausea and Vomiting, and visceral pain. Curr Gastroenterol Rep Feb 2015

Latorre JG Cannabis, Cannabinoids, and Cerebral Metabolism: Potential Applications in Stroke and Disorders of the Central Nervous System. Curr Cardiol Rep Aug 2015

Chakrabarti B Endocannabinoid Signaling in Autism. Neurotherapeutics July 2015

Hepburn CY 17 Cannabidiol as an anti-arrhythmic, the role of the CB 1 receptors. Heart 2011:97

Zogopoulos P The antitumor action of cannabinoids on glioma tumorigenesis. Histology and Histopathology Jun 2015

Chapter Nine

Lou Z Neuroprotection Effect is driven Through the Up regulation of CB 1 Receptor in Experimental Autoimmune Enchephalomyelitis. Journal of Molecular Neuroscience Sept 2015

McAllister SD The Antitumor Activity of Plant-Derived Non-psychoactive Cannabinoids. Journal of Neuroimmune Pharmacology April 2015

Cabral GA Turning Over a New Leaf: Cannabinoid and Endocannabinoid Modulation of Immune Function. J Neuroimmune Pharmacology June 2015

Abrams DJ Cannabis in Cancer Care. Clinical Pharmacology and Therapeutics Apr 2015

Fowler CJ Delta9-tetrahydrocannabinol and cannabidiol as potential curative agents for cancer. May 2015

Chapter Ten

Svendsen KB Does the cannabinoid dronabinol reduce central pain in multiple sclerosis? BMJ 16 July 2004

Zajicek JP Cannabinoids in multiple sclerosis (CAMS) study: safety and efficacy data for 12 months follow up. J Neuro Neurosurg Psychiatry 2005:76

Chiurchiu V Cannabinoid Signaling and Neuroinflammatory Diseases: A melting pot for the Regulation of Brain Immune Responses. Journal of Neuroimmune Pharmacology June 2015

Capral GA Emerging Role of the CB 2 Cannabinoid Receptor in Immune Regulation and Therapeutic Prospects. Jan 2009

Ashton JC The Cannabinoid CB 2 receptor as a Target for Inflammation-Dependent Neurodegeneration. Curr Neuropharmacol Jun 2007

Notcutt WG Clinical use of Cannabinoids for Symptom control in Multiple Sclerosis. Neurotherapeutics Aug 2015

Leocani L Sativex and clinical-neurophysiological measurements of spasticity in Progressive Multiple Sclerosis. J Neurol Aug 2015

Chapter Eleven

Frankel JP Marijuana for Parkinson's tremor Editorial J of Neurology, Neurosurgery and Psychiatry 1990, 53

Ahmed AIA Cannabinoids in late-onset Alzheimer's. Clinical Pharmacology and Therapeutics Apr 2015

Lotan I Cannabis (medical marijuana) treatment for motor and non-motor symptoms of Parkinson's disease: an open label observational study. Clin Neuropharmacol Mar-Apr 2014

Detyniecki K Marijuana Use in Epilepsy: The Myth and the Reality. Current Neurol Neurosci Rep Aug 2015

Celina LS Cannabinoids for the treatment of Agitation and Aggression in Alzheimer's disease. CNS Drugs Aug 2015

Catlow B Cannabinoids for the Treatment of Movement Disorders. Curr Treat Options Neurol July 2015

More SV Promising cannabinoid-based therapies for Parkinson's disease: motor symptoms to neuroprotection. Molecular Neurodegeneration 2015, 10:17

Ibeas C Molecular Targets of Cannabidiol in Neurological Disorders. Neurotherapeutics Aug 2015

Chapter Twelve

Ware MA Smoked cannabis on chronic neuropathic pain: a randomized controlled trial CMAJ 2010; 182

Wisey B A randomized, placebo controlled trial, cross over trial of cannabis cigarettes in neuropathic pain. J Pain 2008; 9

Berman JS Efficacy of two cannabis based medical extracts for relief of central neuropathic pain from brachial plexus avulsion. Pain 2004; 112

Rog DJ Randomized controlled trial of cannabis based medicine in central pain in Multiple Sclerosis. Neurology 2005; 68

Nurmikko TJ Sativex successfully treats neuropathic pain characterized by allodynia. Pain 2007; 133

Langford RM A double-blind randomized, placebo-controlled, parallel group study of THC/CBD oromucosal spray in combination with the existing treatment regimen , in the relief of central neuropathic pain in patients with Multiple Sclerosis. J Neurol 2013; 260

Chapter Thirteen

Mashiah M. Medical cannabis as treatment for chronic combat PTSD, presented at the 2012 Patients Out of Time conference

Greer GR PTSD symposium reports of patients evaluated for the New Mexico Medical Cannabis program J Psychoactive Drugs 2014; 40

Chapter Fourteen

Goldsmith RS Medical Marijuana in the workplace: challenges and management options for occupational physicians. J Occup Environ Med May 2015

Rigguci S Effect of high-potency cannabis on corpus callosum microstructure. PsychologicalMedicine Nov 2015

Forti MD Daily use, Especially of High-potency Cannabis, Drives the Earlier Onset of Psychosis on Cannabis Users. Schizophrenia Bulletin 6 Dec 2013

Drug War Facts.org

National Workrights Institute: Drug Testing in the workplace

Drug Testing Book all about drug testing

Chapter Fifteen

Morral AR Reassessing the marijuana gateway effect. Addiction Dec 2012

Szalavitz M Marijuana as a gateway drug: The myth that will not die. TIMEHealth Oct 2010

Scharff C Marijuana: The Gateway Drug Myth. Psychology Today Aug 2014

Hall WD Is cannabis a gateway drug? Testing hypotheses about the relationship between cannabis use and the use of other illicit drugs. Drug and Alcohol Review v. 24 Issue1 2005

Kandel DB Does marijuana use cause the use of other drugs? JAMA Editorial Jan 2003

Chapter Sixteen

Stea JN Recovery from cannabis Use Disorders: Abstinence versus Moderation and Treatment-assisted Recovery versus Natural Recovery. Psychology of Additive Behaviors. July 13, 2015

Allsop DJ Cannabinoid replacement therapy (CRT): Nabiximols (Sativex) as a novel treatment for cannabis withdrawal. Pharmacometrics and Systems Pharmacology April, 2015

National Institute on Drug Abuse: Is marijuana addictive

Chapter Seventeen

None

Chapter Eighteen

None